The Ultimate Plant Based

Cookbook for Beginners

1600 Days Healthy and Easy Plant Based Recipes to Achieve Balance and Harmony in Your Diet and Life, 30 Days Meal Plan to Revolutionize Your Lifestyle

Elise Heath

CONTENTS

Legumes, Rice & Grains 50

Other Favorites 63

Sauces & Condiments

Desserts & Sweet Treats

Introduction

Hello, I'm thrilled to present to you "The Ultimate Plant Based Cookbook for Beginners". My name is Elise Heath, and I am a passionate advocate of plant-based eating. After experiencing the transformative power of a plant-based diet in my own life, I felt compelled to share my knowledge and recipes with others who are starting their plant-based journey.

This cookbook is not just about providing delicious and easy-to-follow plant-based recipes, but it aims to inspire and guide beginners towards achieving balance and harmony in their diet and life. As a beginner-friendly resource, it is designed to make the transition to a plant-based lifestyle seamless and enjoyable.

In this cookbook, you will find a comprehensive 30-day meal plan that takes the guesswork out of planning your daily meals. It provides a roadmap to help you effortlessly incorporate plant-based foods into your daily routine. Each recipe is carefully crafted to be both healthy and delicious, ensuring that you never feel deprived or bored.

With over 1600 days' worth of plant-based recipes, this cookbook offers a wide variety of flavors and cuisines to keep your taste buds excited. From hearty breakfast options to satisfying main courses and delectable desserts, there is something for everyone. Moreover, the recipes are designed to be simple and easy to prepare, making them accessible to even the most novice of cooks.

By following the recipes and meal plan in this book, you can expect to experience numerous benefits. Not only will you improve your overall health and well-being, but you will also enhance your energy levels, support weight management, and potentially reduce the risk of chronic diseases. "The Ultimate Plant Based Cookbook for Beginners" is not just a collection of recipes; it is a guide to transforming your lifestyle. It is my hope that through this book, you will discover the joy and abundance that comes from plant-based eating. Get ready to revolutionize your lifestyle and embark on a journey towards optimal health and wellness.

So, are you ready to take the first step towards a plant-based lifestyle? Let's dive into the world of plant-based cooking and unlock the endless possibilities that await you. Happy cooking and enjoy the incredible benefits that this cookbook has to offer!

What does the term "Plant-based Diet" refer to?

The term "plant-based diet" refers to an eating pattern that emphasizes whole, minimally processed foods derived from plants. This diet primarily consists of fruits, vegetables, whole grains, legumes, nuts, and seeds. While the focus is on plant foods, individuals following a plant-based diet may still include small amounts of animal products, such as meat, dairy, and eggs, but these are typically consumed in smaller quantities compared to a traditional Western diet. The main principle of a plant-based diet is to prioritize plant foods for their nutritional benefits, while minimizing or eliminating the consumption of highly processed foods, added sugars, and unhealthy fats. It is a flexible approach that can be tailored to individual preferences and health goals. The plant-based diet is not synonymous with being vegan or vegetarian, as it allows for some animal products if desired. However, the emphasis is on plant foods as the foundation of the diet for optimal health and environmental sustainability.

Is a Plant-based Diet the same as being Vegan or Vegetarian?

While a plant-based diet shares similarities with vegan and vegetarian diets, they are not exactly the same.

A vegan diet is a type of plant-based diet that excludes all animal products, including meat, dairy, eggs, and honey. It is a lifestyle choice that extends beyond dietary preferences and typically encompasses avoiding the use of any animal-derived products, such as leather or wool.

On the other hand, a vegetarian diet is also a plant-based diet, but it allows for the consumption of certain animal products, depending on the type of vegetarianism followed. For example, lacto-vegetarians include dairy products in their diet, while ovo-vegetarians consume eggs. Lacto-ovo vegetarians include both dairy and eggs in their diet. Some vegetarians may also choose to include certain types of seafood, such as fish or shellfish (known as pescatarians), while still avoiding other meats.

In contrast, a plant-based diet places the primary focus on consuming whole, minimally processed plant foods, while minimizing or eliminating the intake of animal products. While some individuals following a plant-based diet may choose to exclude all animal products, others may include small amounts of animal products on occasion.

The key difference between a plant-based diet and vegan or vegetarian diets lies in the flexibility and individual interpretation. Plant-based diets can be customized to meet individual needs and preferences, allowing for a more varied approach to incorporating plant foods while still leaving room for occasional consumption of animal products, if desired.

Ultimately, all three diets - plant-based, vegan, and vegetarian - promote the consumption of plant foods as the foundation of a healthy and sustainable diet, while differing in the extent to which animal products are included or excluded.

What are the health benefits of following a Plant-based Diet?

Following a plant-based diet can offer numerous health benefits. Here are some of the key advantages:

- **Reduced risk of chronic diseases**

Plant-based diets have been linked to a lower risk of chronic conditions such as heart disease, high blood pressure, type 2 diabetes, and certain types of cancer. This is primarily due to the high intake of fiber, antioxidants, vitamins, minerals, and phytochemicals found in plant foods.

- **Improved heart health**

Plant-based diets are typically low in saturated fats and cholesterol, which are commonly found in animal products. By reducing or eliminating these dietary components, plant-based diets can help lower cholesterol levels, decrease blood pressure, and reduce the risk of heart disease and stroke.

- **Weight management**

Plant-based diets are often associated with lower body weight and a reduced risk of obesity. Plant foods are generally lower in calories and higher in fiber, which can help promote feelings of fullness and reduce overeating. Additionally, plant-based diets tend to be rich in nutrient-dense foods, which can support weight loss and maintenance.

- **Improved digestion**

Plant-based diets are naturally high in dietary fiber, which promotes healthy digestion and regular bowel movements. Adequate fiber intake can help prevent constipation, promote a healthy gut microbiome, and reduce the risk of gastrointestinal conditions such as diverticulosis and hemorrhoids.

- **Increased nutrient intake**

Plant-based diets can provide a wide range of essential nutrients, including vitamins (such as vitamin C, vitamin E, and folate), minerals (such as potassium, magnesium, and calcium), and antioxidants. By consuming a variety of plant foods, individuals can ensure they meet their nutritional needs and support overall health and vitality.

- **Enhanced immune function**

Plant foods are rich in immune-boosting nutrients, such as vitamin C, vitamin A, and antioxidants. A well-balanced plant-based diet can strengthen the immune system, reduce the risk of infections, and support faster recovery from illnesses.

- **Reduced inflammation**

Chronic inflammation is associated with various diseases, including heart disease, diabetes, and certain types of cancer. Plant-based diets, particularly those rich in fruits, vegetables, whole grains, and healthy fats, can help reduce inflammation in the body due to their anti-inflammatory properties.

- **Better environmental sustainability**

Plant-based diets have a lower carbon footprint compared to diets high in animal products. By reducing the consumption of animal products, individuals can contribute to environmental sustainability and the preservation of natural resources.

It's important to note that while plant-based diets offer many health benefits, it is still essential to ensure a well-balanced and varied diet that includes a wide range of plant foods to meet individual nutrient needs.

Can a Plant-based Diet provide all the necessary nutrients?

Yes, a well-planned and balanced plant-based diet can provide all the necessary nutrients for optimal health. Here's a breakdown of key nutrients and how they can be obtained on a plant-based diet:

- **Protein**

Plant-based protein sources include legumes (beans, lentils, chickpeas), tofu, tempeh, seitan, edamame, quinoa, nuts, seeds, and whole grains. Consuming a variety of these protein-rich foods throughout the day can ensure sufficient protein intake. Combining different plant protein sources can also help improve the quality of protein intake.

- **Iron**

Plant-based iron sources include legumes, tofu, tempeh, spinach, kale, Swiss chard, fortified cereals, quinoa, pumpkin seeds, and dried fruits. Pairing iron-rich foods with vitamin C sources (citrus fruits, bell peppers, broccoli) can enhance iron absorption.

- **Calcium**

Plant-based calcium sources include fortified plant-based milk alternatives (soy, almond, oat), tofu made with calcium sulfate, leafy greens (kale, collard greens, bok choy), broccoli, fortified orange juice, and calcium-set tofu. It's important to ensure adequate intake of calcium-rich foods or consider calcium supplementation if needed.

- **Vitamin B12**

Vitamin B12 is naturally found primarily in animal products. Therefore, individuals following a plant-based diet, especially vegans, should consider fortified foods (plant-based milk, breakfast cereals, nutritional yeast) or B12 supplements to meet their needs.

- **Omega-3 fatty acids**

Plant-based sources of omega-3s include flaxseeds, chia seeds, hemp seeds, walnuts, and algae-based supplements. Consuming these foods regularly can provide the essential omega-3 fatty acids, including alpha-linolenic acid (ALA), which the body can convert to other beneficial omega-3s like EPA and DHA.

- **Vitamin D**

Vitamin D can be obtained from sunlight exposure, fortified plant-based milk alternatives, fortified cereals, and supplements. It may be challenging to obtain sufficient vitamin D from diet alone, especially for individuals with limited sun exposure, so supplementation may be necessary.

- **Zinc**

Plant-based zinc sources include legumes, whole grains, nuts, seeds, and fortified foods. Ensuring a variety of these foods in the diet can help meet zinc requirements.

It's important to note that some individuals, such as pregnant or lactating women, infants, children, and older adults, may have higher nutrient needs or specific considerations.

Breakfast & Smoothies

Spicy Vegetable And Chickpea Tofu Scramble

Servings: 2
Cooking Time: 15 Minutes
Ingredients:

- 2 tablespoons oil
- 1 bell pepper, seeded and sliced
- 2 tablespoons scallions, chopped
- 6 ounces cremini button mushrooms, sliced
- 1/2 teaspoon garlic, minced
- 1 jalapeno pepper, seeded and chopped
- 6 ounces firm tofu, pressed
- 1 tablespoon nutritional yeast
- 1/4 teaspoon turmeric powder
- Kala namak and ground black pepper, to taste
- 6 ounces chickpeas, drained

Directions:

1. Heat the olive oil in a nonstick skillet over a moderate flame. Once hot, sauté the pepper for about 2 minutes.
2. Now, add in the scallions, mushrooms and continue sautéing for a further 3 minutes or until the mushrooms release the liquid.
3. Then, add in the garlic, jalapeno and tofu and sauté for 5 minutes more, crumbling the tofu with a fork.
4. Add in the nutritional yeast, turmeric, salt, pepper and chickpeas; continue sautéing an additional 2 minutes or until cooked through. Bon appétit!

Pecan & Pumpkin Seed Oat Jars

Servings:5
Cooking Time:10 Minutes + Chilling Time
Ingredients:

- 2 ½ cups old-fashioned rolled oats
- 5 tbsp pumpkin seeds
- 5 tbsp chopped pecans
- 5 cups unsweetened soy milk
- 2 ½ tsp agave syrup
- Salt to taste
- 1 tsp ground cardamom
- 1 tsp ground ginger

Directions:

1. In a bowl, put oats, pumpkin seeds, pecans, soy milk, agave syrup, salt, cardamom, and ginger and toss to combine. Divide the mixture between mason jars. Seal the lids and transfer to the fridge to soak for 10-12 hours.

Raspberry Almond Smoothie

Servings:4
Cooking Time:5 Minutes
Ingredients:

- 1 ½ cups almond milk
- ½ cup raspberries
- Juice from half lemon
- ½ tsp almond extract

Directions:

1. In a blender or smoothie maker, pour the almond milk, raspberries, lemon juice, and almond extract. Puree the ingredients at high speed until the raspberries have blended almost entirely into the liquid. Pour the smoothie into serving glasses. Stick in some straws and serve immediately.

Banana-strawberry Smoothie

Servings:4
Cooking Time:5 Minutes
Ingredients:
- 4 bananas, sliced
- 4 cups strawberries
- 4 cups kale
- 4 cups plant-based milk

Directions:
1. In a food processor, add bananas, strawberries, kale, and milk and blitz until smooth. Divide between glasses and serve.

Strawberry & Pecan Breakfast

Servings:2
Cooking Time:15 Minutes
Ingredients:
- 1 can coconut milk, refrigerated overnight
- 1 cup granola
- ½ cup pecans, chopped
- 1 cup sliced strawberries

Directions:
1. Drain the coconut milk liquid. Layer the coconut milk solids, granola, and strawberries in small glasses. Top with chopped pecans and serve right away.

Broccoli Hash Browns

Servings:4
Cooking Time:35 Minutes
Ingredients:
- 3 tbsp flax seed powder
- 1 head broccoli, cut into florets
- ½ white onion, grated
- 1 tsp salt
- 1 tbsp freshly ground black pepper
- 5 tbsp plant butter, for frying

Directions:
1. In a small bowl, mix the flax seed powder with 9 tbsp water, and allow soaking for 5 minutes. Pour the broccoli into a food processor and pulse a few times until smoothly grated.
2. Transfer the broccoli into a bowl, add the vegan "flax egg," white onion, salt, and black pepper. Use a spoon to mix the ingredients evenly and set aside 5 to 10 minutes to firm up a bit. Place a large non-stick skillet over medium heat and drop 1/3 of the plant butter to melt until no longer shimmering.
3. Ladle scoops of the broccoli mixture into the skillet. Flatten the pancakes to measure 3 to 4 inches in diameter, and fry until golden brown on one side, 4 minutes. Turn the pancakes with a spatula and cook the other side to brown too, another 5 minutes.
4. Transfer the hash browns to a serving plate and repeat the frying process for the remaining broccoli mixture. Serve the hash browns warm with green salad.

Morning Oats With Walnuts And Currants

Servings: 2
Cooking Time: 10 Minutes
Ingredients:

- 1 cup water
- 1 ½ cups oat milk
- 1 ½ cups rolled oats
- A pinch of salt
- A pinch of grated nutmeg
- 1/4 teaspoon cardamom
- 1 handful walnuts, roughly chopped
- 4 tablespoons dried currants

Directions:

1. In a deep saucepan, bring the water and milk to a rolling boil. Add in the oats, cover the saucepan and turn the heat to medium.
2. Add in the salt, nutmeg and cardamom. Continue to cook for about 12 to 13 minutes more, stirring occasionally.
3. Spoon the mixture into serving bowls; top with walnuts and currants. Bon appétit!

Cinnamon Semolina Porridge

Servings: 3
Cooking Time: 20 Minutes
Ingredients:

- 3 cups almond milk
- 3 tablespoons maple syrup
- 3 teaspoons coconut oil
- 1/4 teaspoon kosher salt
- 1/2 teaspoon ground cinnamon
- 1 ¼ cups semolina

Directions:

1. In a saucepan, heat the almond milk, maple syrup, coconut oil, salt and cinnamon over a moderate flame.
2. Once hot, gradually stir in the semolina flour. Turn the heat to a simmer and continue cooking until the porridge reaches your preferred consistency.
3. Garnish with your favorite toppings and serve warm. Bon appétit!

Classic Applesauce Pancakes With Coconut

Servings: 8
Cooking Time: 50 Minutes
Ingredients:

- 1 ¼ cups whole-wheat flour
- 1 teaspoon baking powder
- 1/4 teaspoon sea salt
- 1/2 teaspoon coconut sugar
- 1/4 teaspoon ground cloves
- 1/4 teaspoon ground cardamom
- 1/2 teaspoon ground cinnamon
- 3/4 cup oat milk
- 1/2 cup applesauce, unsweetened
- 2 tablespoons coconut oil
- 8 tablespoons coconut, shredded
- 8 tablespoons pure maple syrup

Directions:

1. In a mixing bowl, thoroughly combine the flour, baking powder, salt, sugar and spices. Gradually add in the milk and applesauce.
2. Heat a frying pan over a moderately high flame and add a small amount of the coconut oil.
3. Once hot, pour the batter into the frying pan. Cook for approximately 3 minutes until the bubbles form; flip it and cook on the other side for 3 minutes longer until browned on the underside. Repeat with the remaining oil and batter.
4. Serve with shredded coconut and maple syrup. Bon appétit!

Traditional Spanish Tortilla

Servings: 2
Cooking Time: 35 Minutes
Ingredients:

- 3 tablespoons olive oil
- 2 medium potatoes, peeled and diced
- 1/2 white onion, chopped
- 8 tablespoons gram flour
- 8 tablespoons water
- Sea salt and ground black pepper, to season
- 1/2 teaspoon Spanish paprika

Directions:

1. Heat 2 tablespoons of the olive oil in a frying pan over a moderate flame. Now, cook the potatoes and onion; cook for about 20 minutes or until tender; reserve.
2. In a mixing bowl, thoroughly combine the flour, water, salt, black pepper and paprika. Add in the potato/onion mixture.
3. Heat the remaining 1 tablespoon of the olive oil in the same frying pan. Pour 1/2 of the batter into the frying pan. Cook your tortilla for about 11 minutes, turning it once or twice to promote even cooking.
4. Repeat with the remaining batter and serve warm.

Almond Oatmeal Porridge

Servings:4
Cooking Time:25 Minutes
Ingredients:

- 2 ½ cups vegetable broth
- 2 ½ cups almond milk
- ½ cup steel-cut oats
- 1 tbsp pearl barley
- ½ cup slivered almonds
- ¼ cup nutritional yeast
- 2 cups old-fashioned rolled oats

Directions:

1. Pour the broth and almond milk in a pot over medium heat and bring to a boil. Stir in oats, pearl barley, almond slivers, and nutritional yeast. Reduce the heat and simmer for 20 minutes. Add in the rolled oats, cook for an additional 5 minutes, until creamy. Allow cooling before serving.

Pumpkin Cake With Pistachios

Servings:4
Cooking Time:70 Minutes
Ingredients:

- 2 tbsp flaxseed powder
- 3 tbsp vegetable oil
- ¾ cup canned pumpkin puree
- ½ cup pure corn syrup
- 3 tbsp pure date sugar
- 1 ½ cups whole-wheat flour
- ½ tsp cinnamon powder
- ½ tsp baking powder
- ¼ tsp cloves powder
- ½ tsp allspice powder
- ½ tsp nutmeg powder
- 2 tbsp chopped pistachios

Directions:

1. Preheat the oven to 350°F and lightly coat an 8 x 4-inch loaf pan with cooking spray. In a bowl, mix the flax seed powder with 6 tbsp water and allow thickening for 5 minutes to make the vegan "flax egg."
2. In a bowl, whisk the vegetable oil, pumpkin puree, corn syrup, date sugar, and vegan "flax egg." In another bowl, mix the flour, cinnamon powder, baking powder, cloves powder, allspice powder, and nutmeg powder. Add this mixture to the wet batter and mix until well combined. Pour the batter into the loaf pan, sprinkle the pistachios on top, and gently press the nuts onto the batter to stick.
3. Bake in the oven for 50-55 minutes or until a toothpick inserted into the cake comes out clean. Remove the cake onto a wire rack, allow cooling, slice, and serve.

Buckwheat Porridge With Apples And Almonds

Servings: 3
Cooking Time: 20 Minutes
Ingredients:

- 1 cup buckwheat groats, toasted
- 3/4 cup water
- 1 cup rice milk
- 1/4 teaspoon sea salt
- 3 tablespoons agave syrup
- 1 cup apples, cored and diced
- 3 tablespoons almonds, slivered
- 2 tablespoons coconut flakes
- 2 tablespoons hemp seeds

Directions:

1. In a saucepan, bring the buckwheat groats, water, milk and salt to a boil. Immediately turn the heat to a simmer; let it simmer for about 13 minutes until it has softened.
2. Stir in the agave syrup. Divide the porridge between three serving bowls.
3. Garnish each serving with the apples, almonds, coconut and hemp seeds. Bon appétit!

Maple Banana Oats

Servings:4
Cooking Time:35 Minutes
Ingredients:

- 3 cups water
- 1 cup steel-cut oats
- 2 bananas, mashed
- ¼ cup pumpkin seeds
- 2 tbsp maple syrup
- A pinch of salt

Directions:

1. Bring water to a boil in a pot, add in oats, and lower the heat. Cook for 20-30 minutes. Put in the mashed bananas, cook for 3-5 minutes more. Stir in maple syrup, pumpkin seeds, and salt. Serve.

Morning Kasha With Mushrooms

Servings: 2
Cooking Time: 30 Minutes
Ingredients:

- 1 cup water
- 1/2 cup buckwheat groats, toasted
- Sea salt and ground black pepper, to taste
- 2 tablespoons olive oil
- 1 cup button mushrooms, sliced
- 2 tablespoons scallions, chopped
- 1 garlic clove, minced
- 1 small avocado, pitted, peeled and sliced
- 1 tablespoon fresh lemon juice

Directions:

1. In a saucepan, bring the water and buckwheat to a boil. Immediately turn the heat to a simmer and continue to cook for about 20 minutes. Season with sea salt and ground black pepper to taste.
2. Then, heat the olive oil in a nonstick skillet, over medium-high heat. Sauté the mushrooms, scallions and garlic for about 4 minutes or until they've softened.
3. Spoon the kasha into two serving bowls; top each serving with the sautéed mushroom mixture.
4. Garnish with avocado, add a few drizzles of fresh lemon juice and serve immediately. Bon appétit!

Thyme Pumpkin Stir-fry

Servings:2
Cooking Time:25 Minutes
Ingredients:
- 1 cup pumpkin, shredded
- 1 tbsp olive oil
- ½ onion, chopped
- 1 carrot, peeled and chopped
- 2 garlic cloves, minced
- ½ tsp dried thyme
- 1 cup chopped kale
- Salt and black pepper to taste

Directions:
1. Heat the oil in a skillet over medium heat. Sauté onion and carrot for 5 minutes. Add in garlic and thyme, cook for 30 seconds until the garlic is fragrant. Place in the pumpkin and cook for 10 minutes until tender. Stir in kale, cook for 4 minutes until the kale wilts. Season with salt and pepper. Serve hot.

Berry Quinoa Bowl

Servings:4
Cooking Time:5 Minutes
Ingredients:
- 3 cups cooked quinoa
- 1 ⅓ cups unsweetened almond milk
- 2 bananas, sliced
- 2 cups berries
- ½ cup chopped raw hazelnuts
- ¼ cup agave syrup

Directions:
1. In a large bowl, combine the quinoa, milk, banana, raspberries, blueberries, and hazelnuts. Divide between serving bowls and top with agave syrup to serve.

Chocolate-mango Quinoa Bowl

Servings:2
Cooking Time:35 Minutes
Ingredients:
- 1 cup quinoa
- 1 tsp ground cinnamon
- 1 cup non-dairy milk
- 1 large mango, chopped
- 3 tbsp unsweetened cocoa powder
- 2 tbsp almond butter
- 1 tbsp hemp seeds
- 1 tbsp walnuts
- ¼ cup raspberries

Directions:
1. In a pot, combine the quinoa, cinnamon, milk, and 1 cup of water over medium heat. Bring to a boil, low heat, and simmer covered for 25-30 minutes. In a bowl, mash the mango and mix cocoa powder, almond butter, and hemp seeds. In a serving bowl, place cooked quinoa and mango mixture. Top with walnuts and raspberries. Serve immediately.

Creamy Sesame Bread

Servings:6
Cooking Time:40 Minutes
Ingredients:
- 4 tbsp flax seed powder
- 2/3 cup cashew cream cheese
- 4 tbsp sesame oil + for brushing
- 1 cup coconut flour
- 2 tbsp psyllium husk powder
- 1 tsp salt
- 1 tsp baking powder
- 1 tbsp sesame seeds

Directions:
1.   In a bowl, mix the flax seed powder with 1 ½ cups water until smoothly combined and set aside to soak for 5 minutes. Preheat oven to 400°F. When the vegan "flax egg" is ready, beat in the cream cheese and sesame oil until well mixed.
2.   Whisk in the coconut flour, psyllium husk powder, salt, and baking powder until adequately blended.
3.   Grease a 9 x 5 inches baking tray with cooking spray, and spread the dough in the tray. Allow the mixture to stand for 5 minutes and then brush with some sesame oil.
4.   Sprinkle with the sesame seeds and bake the dough for 30 minutes or until golden brown on top and set within. Take out the bread and allow cooling for a few minutes. Slice and serve.

Veggie Panini

Servings:4
Cooking Time:30 Minutes
Ingredients:
- 1 tbsp olive oil
- 1 cup sliced button mushrooms
- Salt and black pepper to taste
- 1 ripe avocado, sliced
- 2 tbsp freshly squeezed lemon juice
- 1 tbsp chopped parsley
- ½ tsp pure maple syrup
- 8 slices whole-wheat ciabatta
- 4 oz sliced plant-based Parmesan

Directions:
1.   Heat the olive oil in a medium skillet over medium heat and sauté the mushrooms until softened, 5 minutes. Season with salt and black pepper. Turn the heat off.
2.   Preheat a panini press to medium heat, 3 to 5 minutes. Mash the avocado in a medium bowl and mix in the lemon juice, parsley, and maple syrup. Spread the mixture on 4 bread slices, divide the mushrooms and plant-based Parmesan cheese on top. Cover with the other bread slices and brush the top with olive oil. Grill the sandwiches one after another in the heated press until golden brown, and the cheese is melted. Serve.

Vanilla Crepes With Berry Cream Compote Topping

Servings:4
Cooking Time:35 Minutes
Ingredients:

- For the berry cream:
- 2 tbsp plant butter
- 2 tbsp pure date sugar
- 1 tsp vanilla extract
- ½ cup fresh blueberries
- ½ cup fresh raspberries
- ½ cup whipped coconut cream
- For the crepes:
- 2 tbsp flax seed powder
- 1 tsp vanilla extract
- 1 tsp pure date sugar
- ¼ tsp salt
- 2 cups almond flour
- 1 ½ cups almond milk
- 1 ½ cups water
- 3 tbsp plant butter for frying

Directions:

1. Melt butter in a pot over low heat and mix in the date sugar, and vanilla. Cook until the sugar melts and then toss in berries. Allow softening for 2-3 minutes. Set aside to cool.

2. In a medium bowl, mix the flax seed powder with 6 tbsp water and allow to thicken for 5 minutes to make the vegan "flax egg." Whisk in vanilla, date sugar, and salt. Pour in a quarter cup of almond flour and whisk, then a quarter cup of almond milk, and mix until no lumps remain. Repeat the mixing process with the remaining almond flour and almond milk in the same quantities until exhausted.

3. Mix in 1 cup of water until the mixture is runny like that of pancakes, and add the remaining water until it is lighter. Brush a large non-stick skillet with some butter and place over medium heat to melt. Pour 1 tablespoon of the batter into the pan and swirl the skillet quickly and all around to coat the pan with the batter. Cook until the batter is dry and golden brown beneath, about 30 seconds.

4. Use a spatula to carefully flip the crepe and cook the other side until golden brown too. Fold the crepe onto a plate and set aside. Repeat making more crepes with the remaining batter until exhausted. Plate the crepes, top with the whipped coconut cream and the berry compote. Serve immediately.

Simple Apple Muffins

Servings:4
Cooking Time:40 Minutes
Ingredients:

- For the muffins:
- 1 flax seed powder + 3 tbsp water
- 1 ½ cups whole-wheat flour
- ¾ cup pure date sugar
- 2 tsp baking powder
- ¼ tsp salt
- 1 tsp cinnamon powder
- 1/3 cup melted plant butter
- 1/3 cup flax milk
- 2 apples, chopped
- For topping:
- 1/3 cup whole-wheat flour
- ½ cup pure date sugar
- ½ cup cold plant butter, cubed
- 1 ½ tsp cinnamon powder

Directions:

1. Preheat oven to 400°F and grease 6 muffin cups with cooking spray. In a bowl, mix the flax seed powder with water and allow thickening for 5 minutes to make the vegan "flax egg."

2. In a bowl, mix flour, date sugar, baking powder, salt, and cinnamon powder. Whisk in the butter, vegan "flax egg," flax milk, and fold in the apples. Fill the muffin cups two-thirds way up with the batter.

3. In a bowl, mix remaining flour, date sugar, cold butter, and cinnamon powder. Sprinkle the mixture on the muffin batter. Bake for 20 minutes. Remove the muffins onto a wire rack, allow cooling, and serve.

Amazing Yellow Smoothie

Servings:4
Cooking Time:5 Minutes
Ingredients:
- 1 banana
- 1 cup chopped mango
- 1 cup chopped apricots
- 1 cup strawberries
- 1 carrot, peeled and chopped
- 1 cup water

Directions:
1. Put the banana, mango, apricots, strawberries, carrot, and water in a food processor. Pulse until smooth; add more water if needed. Divide between glasses and serve.

Coconut Fruit Smoothie

Servings:3
Cooking Time:5 Minutes
Ingredients:
- 1 cup strawberries
- 1 cup chopped watermelon
- 1 cup cranberries
- 1 tbsp chia seeds
- ½ cup coconut milk
- 1 cup water
- 1 tsp goji berries
- 2 tbsp fresh mint, chopped

Directions:
1. In a food processor, put the strawberries, watermelon, cranberries, chia seeds, coconut milk, water, goji berries, and mint. Pulse until smooth, adding more water or milk if needed. Divide between 3 glasses and serve.

Gingerbread Belgian Waffles

Servings: 3
Cooking Time: 25 Minutes
Ingredients:
- 1 cup all-purpose flour
- 1 teaspoon baking powder
- 1 tablespoon brown sugar
- 1 teaspoon ground ginger
- 1 cup almond milk
- 1 teaspoon vanilla extract
- 2 olive oil

Directions:
1. Preheat a waffle iron according to the manufacturer's instructions.
2. In a mixing bowl, thoroughly combine the flour, baking powder, brown sugar, ground ginger, almond milk, vanilla extract and olive oil.
3. Beat until everything is well blended.
4. Ladle 1/3 of the batter into the preheated waffle iron and cook until the waffles are golden and crisp. Repeat with the remaining batter.
5. Serve your waffles with blackberry jam, if desired. Bon appétit!

Tropical French Toasts

Servings: 4
Cooking Time: 55 Minutes

Ingredients:

- 2 tbsp flax seed powder
- 1 ½ cups unsweetened almond milk
- ½ cup almond flour
- 2 tbsp maple syrup + extra for drizzling
- 2 pinches of salt
- ½ tbsp cinnamon powder
- ½ tsp fresh lemon zest
- 1 tbsp fresh pineapple juice
- 8 whole-grain bread slices

Directions:

1. Preheat the oven to 400°F and lightly grease a roasting rack with olive oil. Set aside.
2. In a medium bowl, mix the flax seed powder with 6 tbsp water and allow thickening for 5 to 10 minutes. Whisk in the almond milk, almond flour, maple syrup, salt, cinnamon powder, lemon zest, and pineapple juice. Soak the bread on both sides in the almond milk mixture and allow sitting on a plate for 2 to 3 minutes.
3. Heat a large skillet over medium heat and place the bread in the pan. Cook until golden brown on the bottom side. Flip the bread and cook further until golden brown on the other side, 4 minutes in total. Transfer to a plate, drizzle some maple syrup on top and serve immediately.

Classic French Toast

Servings: 2
Cooking Time: 20 Minutes

Ingredients:

- 1 tablespoon ground flax seeds
- 1 cup coconut milk
- 1/2 teaspoon vanilla paste
- A pinch of sea salt
- A pinch of grated nutmeg
- 1/2 teaspoon ground cinnamon
- 1/4 teaspoon ground cloves
- 1 tablespoon agave syrup
- 4 slices bread

Directions:

1. In a mixing bowl, thoroughly combine the flax seeds, coconut milk, vanilla, salt, nutmeg, cinnamon, cloves and agave syrup.
2. Dredge each slice of bread into the milk mixture until well coated on all sides.
3. Preheat an electric griddle to medium heat and lightly oil it with a nonstick cooking spray.
4. Cook each slice of bread on the preheated griddle for about 3 minutes per side until golden brown.
5. Bon appétit!

Fluffy Banana Pancakes

Servings: 4
Cooking Time: 25 Minutes
Ingredients:

- 2 tablespoons ground flaxseeds
- 1/2 cup oat flour
- 1/2 cup coconut flour
- 1/2 cup instant oats
- 1 teaspoon baking powder
- 1/4 teaspoon kosher salt
- 1/4 teaspoon ground cardamom
- 1/4 teaspoon ground cinnamon
- 1/2 teaspoon coconut extract
- 1 cup banana
- 2 tablespoons coconut oil, at room temperature

Directions:

1. To make the "flax" egg, in a small mixing dish, whisk 2 tablespoons of the ground flaxseeds with 4 tablespoons of the water. Let it sit for at least 15 minutes.
2. In a mixing bowl, thoroughly combine the flour, oats, baking powder and spices. Add in the flax egg and mashed banana. Mix until everything is well incorporated.
3. Heat 1/2 tablespoon of the coconut oil in a frying pan over medium-low flame. Spoon about 1/4 cup of the batter into the frying pan; fry your pancake for approximately 3 minutes per side.
4. Repeat until you run out of batter. Serve with your favorite fixings and enjoy!

Spicy Apple Pancakes

Servings:4
Cooking Time:30 Minutes
Ingredients:

- 2 cups almond milk
- 1 tsp apple cider vinegar
- 2 ½ cups whole-wheat flour
- 2 tbsp baking powder
- ½ tsp baking soda
- 1 tsp sea salt
- ½ tsp ground cinnamon
- ¼ tsp grated nutmeg
- ¼ tsp ground allspice
- ½ cup applesauce
- 1 cup water
- 1 tbsp coconut oil

Directions:

1. Whisk the almond milk and apple cider vinegar in a bowl and set aside. In another bowl, combine the flour, baking powder, baking soda, salt, cinnamon, nutmeg, and allspice. Transfer the almond mixture to another bowl and beat with the applesauce and water.
2. Pour in the dry ingredients and stir. Melt some coconut oil in a skillet over medium heat. Pour a ladle of the batter and cook for 5 minutes, flipping once until golden. Repeat the process until the batter is exhausted. Serve warm.

Vegan Banh Mi

Servings: 4
Cooking Time: 35 Minutes

Ingredients:

- 1/2 cup rice vinegar
- 1/4 cup water
- 1/4 cup white sugar
- 2 carrots, cut into 1/16-inch-thick matchsticks
- 1/2 cup white (daikon) radish, cut into 1/16-inch-thick matchsticks
- 1 white onion, thinly sliced
- 2 tablespoons olive oil
- 12 ounces firm tofu, cut into sticks
- 1/4 cup vegan mayonnaise
- 1 ½ tablespoons soy sauce
- 2 cloves garlic, minced
- 1/4 cup fresh parsley, chopped
- Kosher salt and ground black pepper, to taste
- 2 standard French baguettes, cut into four pieces
- 4 tablespoons fresh cilantro, chopped
- 4 lime wedges

Directions:

1. Bring the rice vinegar, water and sugar to a boil and stir until the sugar has dissolved, about 1 minute. Allow it to cool.
2. Pour the cooled vinegar mixture over the carrot, daikon radish and onion; allow the vegetables to marinate for at least 30 minutes.
3. While the vegetables are marinating, heat the olive oil in a frying pan over medium-high heat. Once hot, add the tofu and sauté for 8 minutes, stirring occasionally to promote even cooking.
4. Then, mix the mayo, soy sauce, garlic, parsley, salt and ground black pepper in a small bowl.
5. Slice each piece of the baguette in half the long way Then, toast the baguette halves under the preheated broiler for about 3 minutes.
6. To assemble the banh mi sandwiches, spread each half of the toasted baguette with the mayonnaise mixture; fill the cavity of the bottom half of the bread with the fried tofu sticks, marinated vegetables and cilantro leaves.
7. Lastly, squeeze the lime wedges over the filling and top with the other half of the baguette. Bon appétit!

Snacks, Appetizers & Side Dishes

Crispy Mushroom Wontons

Servings:12
Cooking Time:20 Minutes
Ingredients:

- 12 vegan wonton wrappers
- 3 tbsp toasted sesame oil
- 2 tbsp olive oil
- 12 shiitake mushrooms, sliced
- 4 green beans, chopped crosswise
- 1 tsp soy sauce
- 1 tbsp fresh lime juice
- 1 medium carrot, shredded
- Toasted sesame seeds

Directions:

1. Preheat oven to 360°F.
2. Coat the wonton with some sesame oil and arrange on a baking sheet. Put in the oven and bake for 5 minutes until golden brown and crispy. Set aside. Warm the olive oil in a skillet over medium heat. Place the mushrooms and stir-fry for 5 minutes until softened. Add in green beans and soy sauce and cook for 2-3 minutes; reserve.
3. In a bowl, whisk the lime juice and the remaining sesame oil. Stir in carrot and mushroom mixture. Divide the mixture between the wontons and sprinkle with sesame seeds. Serve.

Hummus Avocado Boats

Servings: 4
Cooking Time: 10 Minutes
Ingredients:

- 1 tablespoon fresh lemon juice
- 2 ripe avocados, halved and pitted
- 8 ounces hummus
- 1 garlic clove, minced
- 1 medium tomato, chopped
- Sea salt and ground black pepper, to taste
- 1/2 teaspoon turmeric powder
- 1/2 teaspoon cayenne pepper
- 1 tablespoon tahini

Directions:

1. Drizzle the fresh lemon juice over the avocado halves.
2. Mix the hummus, garlic, tomato, salt, black pepper, turmeric powder, cayenne pepper and tahini. Spoon the filling into your avocados.
3. Serve immediately.

Rosemary And Garlic Roasted Carrots

Servings: 4
Cooking Time: 25 Minutes
Ingredients:

- 2 pounds carrots, trimmed and halved lengthwise
- 4 tablespoons olive oil
- 2 tablespoons champagne vinegar
- 4 cloves garlic, minced
- 2 sprigs rosemary, chopped
- Sea salt and ground black pepper, to taste
- 4 tablespoons pine nuts, chopped

Directions:

1. Begin by preheating your oven to 400°F.
2. Toss the carrots with the olive oil, vinegar, garlic, rosemary, salt and black pepper. Arrange them in a single layer on a parchment-lined roasting sheet.
3. Roast the carrots in the preheated oven for about 20 minutes, until fork-tender.
4. Garnish the carrots with the pine nuts and serve immediately. Bon appétit!

Kale & Hummus Pinwheels

Servings:4
Cooking Time:10 Minutes
Ingredients:
- 3 whole-grain flour tortillas
- 1 cup kale, chopped
- ¾ cup hummus
- ¾ cup shredded carrots

Directions:
1. Spread the hummus over the tortillas and top with kale and carrots. Fold the edges over the filling and roll up to make burritos. Cut into pinwheels and serve.

Hazelnut Snack

Servings:1
Cooking Time:10 Minutes
Ingredients:
- ½ cup raw hazelnuts
- 2 tbsp tamari sauce
- 1 tsp toasted sesame oil

Directions:
1. Heat a skillet over medium heat. Place in hazelnuts and toast for 7-8 minutes, moving continually with a spatula. Stir in tamari sauce and sesame oil to coat. Remove from the heat and allow the tamari mixture to dry on the hazelnuts.

Silky Kohlrabi Puree

Servings: 4
Cooking Time: 30 Minutes
Ingredients:
- 1 ½ pounds kohlrabi, peeled and cut into pieces
- 4 tablespoons vegan butter
- Sea salt and freshly ground black pepper, to taste
- 1/2 teaspoon cumin seeds
- 1/2 teaspoon coriander seeds
- 1/2 cup soy milk
- 1 teaspoon fresh dill
- 1 teaspoon fresh parsley

Directions:
1. Cook the kohlrabi in boiling salted water until soft, about 30 minutes; drain.
2. Puree the kohlrabi with the vegan butter, salt, black pepper, cumin seeds and coriander seeds.
3. Puree the ingredients with an immersion blender, gradually adding the milk. Top with fresh dill and parsley. Bon appétit!

Balkan-style Satarash

Servings: 4
Cooking Time: 25 Minutes
Ingredients:

- 4 tablespoons olive oil
- 1 large onion, chopped
- 1 pound eggplant, peeled and diced
- 2 red bell peppers, seeded and diced
- 1 red chili pepper, seeded and diced
- 2 garlic cloves, minced
- 1 teaspoon paprika, slightly heaping
- 1 bay leaf
- Kosher salt and ground black pepper, to taste
- 1 large tomato, pureed
- 1/2 cup vegetable broth

Directions:
1. Heat the oil in a large saucepan over medium-high flame.
2. Then, sauté the onion for about 3 minutes or until tender and translucent. Add in the eggplant and peppers and continue sautéing an additional 3 minutes.
3. Add in the garlic and continue to cook for 30 seconds more or until aromatic.
4. Add in the remaining ingredients, cover and continue to cook for 15 minutes more or until thoroughly cooked. Serve warm.

Garlic And Herb Mushroom Skillet

Servings: 4
Cooking Time: 10 Minutes
Ingredients:

- 4 tablespoons vegan butter
- 1 ½ pounds oyster mushrooms halved
- 3 cloves garlic, minced
- 1 teaspoon dried oregano
- 1 teaspoon dried rosemary
- 1 teaspoon dried parsley flakes
- 1 teaspoon dried marjoram
- 1/2 cup dry white wine
- Kosher salt and ground black pepper, to taste

Directions:
1. In a sauté pan, heat the olive oil over a moderately high heat.
2. Now, sauté the mushrooms for 3 minutes or until they release the liquid. Add in the garlic and continue to cook for 30 seconds more or until aromatic.
3. Stir in the spices and continue sautéing an additional 6 minutes, until your mushrooms are lightly browned.
4. Bon appétit!

Parmesan Baby Potatoes

Servings:4
Cooking Time:40 Minutes
Ingredients:

- 4 tbsp plant butter, melted
- 4 garlic cloves, minced
- 3 tbsp chopped chives
- Salt and black pepper to taste
- 2 tbsp grated plant-based Parmesan
- 1 ½ lb baby potatoes

Directions:
1. Preheat the oven to 400°F.
2. In a bowl, mix the butter, garlic, chives, salt, pepper, and plant Parmesan cheese. Toss the potatoes in the butter mixture until coated. Spread the mixture into a baking sheet, cover with foil, and roast for 30 minutes. Remove the potatoes from the oven and toss in the remaining butter mixture. Serve.

Tamari Lentil Dip

Servings:2
Cooking Time:10 Minutes
Ingredients:
- 1 can lentils, drained
- Zest and juice of 1 lime
- 1 tbsp tamari sauce
- ¼ cup fresh cilantro, chopped
- 1 tsp ground cumin
- 1 tsp cayenne pepper

Directions:
1. In a blender, put the lentils, lime zest, lime juice, tamari sauce, and ¼ cup of water. Pulse until smooth. Transfer to a bowl and stir in cilantro, cumin and cayenne pepper. Serve.

Wine-braised Kale

Servings: 4
Cooking Time: 10 Minutes
Ingredients:
- 1/2 cup water
- 1 ½ pounds kale
- 3 tablespoons olive oil
- 4 tablespoons scallions, chopped
- 4 cloves garlic, minced
- 1/2 cup dry white wine
- 1/2 teaspoon mustard seeds
- Kosher salt and ground black pepper, to taste

Directions:
1. In a large saucepan, bring the water to a boil. Add in the kale and let it cook until bright, about 3 minutes. Drain and squeeze dry.
2. Wipe the saucepan with paper towels and preheat the olive oil over a moderate heat. Once hot, cook the scallions and garlic for approximately 2 minutes, until they are fragrant.
3. Add in the wine, flowed by the kale, mustard seeds, salt, black pepper; continue to cook, covered, for a further 5 minutes or until heated through.
4. Ladle into individual bowls and serve hot. Bon appétit!

Spinach, Chickpea And Garlic Crostini

Servings: 6
Cooking Time: 10 Minutes
Ingredients:
- 1 baguette, cut into slices
- 4 tablespoons extra-virgin olive oil
- Sea salt and red pepper, to season
- 3 garlic cloves, minced
- 1 cup boiled chickpeas, drained
- 2 cups spinach
- 1 tablespoon fresh lemon juice

Directions:
1. Preheat your broiler.
2. Brush the slices of bread with 2 tablespoons of the olive oil and sprinkle with sea salt and red pepper. Place under the preheated broiler for about 2 minutes or until lightly toasted.
3. In a mixing bowl, thoroughly combine the garlic, chickpeas, spinach, lemon juice and the remaining 2 tablespoons of the olive oil.
4. Spoon the chickpea mixture onto each toast. Bon appétit!

Four-seed Crackers

Servings:4
Cooking Time:50 Minutes
Ingredients:
- 1/3 cup coconut flour
- 1/3 cup sesame seeds
- 1/3 cup sunflower seeds
- 1/3 cup chia seeds
- 1/3 cup pumpkin seeds
- ¼ cup plant butter, melted

Directions:
1. Preheat an oven to 300°F and line a baking sheet with parchment paper.
2. In a bowl, mix the coconut flour, sesame seeds, sunflower seeds, chia seeds, pumpkin seeds, and salt. Add the plant butter, 1 cup of boiling water, and mix until well combined. Spread the mixture on the baking sheet and bake in the oven until the batter is firm, 45 minutes. Remove the crackers and allow cooling for 10 minutes. Break the crackers into pieces and serve.

Mexican-style Onion Rings

Servings: 6
Cooking Time: 35 Minutes
Ingredients:
- 2 medium onions, cut into rings
- 1/4 cup all-purpose flour
- 1/4 cup spelt flour
- 1/3 cup rice milk, unsweetened
- 1/3 cup ale beer
- Sea salt and ground black pepper, to season
- 1/2 teaspoon cayenne pepper
- 1/2 teaspoon mustard seeds
- 1 cup tortilla chips, crushed
- 1 tablespoon olive oil

Directions:
1. Start by preheating your oven to 420°F.
2. In a shallow bowl, mix the flour, milk and beer.
3. In another shallow bowl, mix the spices with the crushed tortilla chips. Dredge the onion rings in the flour mixture.
4. Then, roll them over the spiced mixture, pressing down to coat well.
5. Arrange the onion rings on a parchment-lined baking pan. Brush them with olive oil and bake for approximately 30 minutes. Bon appétit!

Greek-style Eggplant Skillet

Servings: 4
Cooking Time: 15 Minutes
Ingredients:
- 4 tablespoons olive oil
- 1 ½ pounds eggplant, peeled and sliced
- 1 teaspoon garlic, minced
- 1 tomato, crushed
- Sea salt and ground black pepper, to taste
- 1 teaspoon cayenne pepper
- 1/2 teaspoon dried oregano
- 1/4 teaspoon ground bay leaf
- 2 ounces Kalamata olives, pitted and sliced

Directions:
1. Heat the oil in a sauté pan over medium-high flame.
2. Then, sauté the eggplant for about 9 minutes or until just tender.
3. Add in the remaining ingredients, cover and continue to cook for 2 to 3 minutes more or until thoroughly cooked. Serve warm.

Spiced Roasted Cauliflower

Servings: 6
Cooking Time: 25 Minutes
Ingredients:
- 1 ½ pounds cauliflower florets
- 1/4 cup olive oil
- 4 tablespoons apple cider vinegar
- 2 cloves garlic, pressed
- 1 teaspoon dried basil
- 1 teaspoon dried oregano
- Sea salt and ground black pepper, to taste

Directions:
1. Begin by preheating your oven to 420 °F.
2. Toss the cauliflower florets with the remaining ingredients.
3. Arrange the cauliflower florets on a parchment-lined baking sheet. Bake the cauliflower florets in the preheated oven for about 25 minutes or until they are slightly charred.
4. Bon appétit!

Za'atar Roasted Zucchini Sticks

Servings: 5
Cooking Time: 1 Hour 35 Minutes
Ingredients:
- 1 ½ pounds zucchini, cut into sticks lengthwise
- 2 garlic cloves, crushed
- 2 tablespoons extra-virgin olive oil
- 1 teaspoon za'atar spice
- Kosher salt and ground black pepper, to taste

Directions:
1. Toss the zucchini with the remaining ingredients.
2. Lay the zucchini sticks in a single layer on a parchment-lined baking pan.
3. Bake at 235 °F for about 90 minutes until crisp and golden. Zucchini sticks will crisp up as they cool.
4. Bon appétit!

Chipotle Sweet Potato Fries

Servings: 4
Cooking Time: 45 Minutes
Ingredients:
- 4 medium sweet potatoes, peeled and cut into sticks
- 2 tablespoons peanut oil
- Sea salt and ground black pepper, to taste
- 1 teaspoon chipotle pepper powder
- 1/4 teaspoon ground allspice
- 1 teaspoon brown sugar
- 1 teaspoon dried rosemary

Directions:
1. Toss the sweet potato fries with the remaining ingredients.
2. Bake your fries at 375°F for about 45 minutes or until browned; make sure to stir the fries once or twice.
3. Serve with your favorite dipping sauce, if desired. Bon appétit!

Mustard Tofu-avocado Wraps

Servings:4
Cooking Time:25 Minutes
Ingredients:
- 6 tbsp olive oil
- 1 lb extra-firm tofu, cut into strips
- 1 tbsp soy sauce
- ¼ cup apple cider vinegar
- 1 tsp yellow mustard
- 3 cups shredded romaine lettuce
- 3 ripe Roma tomatoes, chopped
- 1 large carrot, shredded
- 1 medium avocado, chopped
- ⅓ cup minced red onion
- ¼ cup sliced pitted green olives
- 4 whole-grain flour tortillas

Directions:
1. Heat 2 tbsp of olive oil in a skillet over medium heat. Place the tofu, cook for 10 minutes until golden brown. Drizzle with soy sauce. Let cool.
2. In a bowl, whisk the vinegar, mustard, salt, pepper, and the remaining oil. In another bowl, mix the lettuce, tomatoes, carrot, avocado, onion, and olives. Pour the dressing over the salad and toss to coat. Lay out a tortilla on a clean flat surface and spoon ¼ of the salad, some tofu, and then roll-up. Cut in half. Repeat the process with the remaining tortillas. Serve.

Arugula & Hummus Pitas

Servings:4
Cooking Time:15 Minutes
Ingredients:
- 4 pieces of whole-wheat pita bread, halved
- 1 garlic clove, chopped
- ¾ cup tahini
- 2 tbsp fresh lemon juice
- ⅛ tsp ground cayenne
- ¼ cup water
- 1 can chickpeas
- 2 medium carrots, grated
- 1 large ripe tomato, sliced
- 2 cups arugula

Directions:
1. In a food processor, add in garlic, tahini, lemon juice, salt, cayenne pepper, and water. Pulse until smooth. In a bowl, mash the chickpeas with a fork. Stir in carrots and tahini mixture; reserve. Spread the hummus over the pitas and top with a tomato slice and arugula. Serve immediately.

Thai Stir-fried Spinach

Servings: 4
Cooking Time: 15 Minutes
Ingredients:
- 2 tablespoons sesame oil
- 1 onion, chopped
- 1 carrot, trimmed and chopped
- 1 Bird's eye chili pepper, minced
- 2 cloves garlic, minced
- 1 ½ pounds spinach leaves, torn into pieces
- 1/3 cup vegetable broth
- 2/3 cup coconut milk, unsweetened

Directions:
1. In a saucepan, heat the sesame oil over medium-high heat.
2. Then, sauté the onion and carrot for about 3 minutes or until tender. Then, sauté the garlic and Bird's eye chili for about 1 minute until aromatic.
3. Add in the broth and spinach and bring to a boil.
4. Turn the heat to a simmer and continue to cook for 5 minutes longer.
5. Add in the coconut milk and simmer for a further 5 minutes or until everything is cooked through. Bon appétit!

Bell Pepper & Seitan Balls

Servings:4
Cooking Time:25 Minutes
Ingredients:
- 1 tbsp flaxseed powder
- 1 lb seitan, crumbled
- ¼ cup chopped mixed bell peppers
- Salt and black pepper to taste
- 1 tbsp almond flour
- 1 tsp garlic powder
- 1 tsp onion powder
- 1 tsp tofu mayonnaise
- Olive oil for brushing

Directions:
1. Preheat the oven to 400°F and line a baking sheet with parchment paper.
2. In a bowl, mix flaxseed powder with 3 tbsp water and allow thickening for 5 minutes. Add in seitan, bell peppers, salt, pepper, almond flour, garlic powder, onion powder, and tofu mayonnaise. Mix and form 1-inch balls from the mixture. Arrange on the baking sheet, brush with cooking spray, and bake in the oven for 15 to 20 minutes or until brown and compacted. Remove from the oven and serve.

Easy Zucchini Skillet

Servings: 4
Cooking Time: 10 Minutes
Ingredients:
- 2 tablespoons vegan butter
- 1 shallot, thinly sliced
- 1 teaspoon garlic, minced
- 1 ½ pounds zucchini, sliced
- Flaky sea salt and ground black pepper, to taste
- 1 teaspoon paprika
- 1/2 teaspoon cayenne pepper
- 1/2 teaspoon dried thyme
- 1/2 teaspoon celery seeds
- 1/2 teaspoon coriander pepper
- 2 tablespoons nutritional yeast

Directions:
1. In a saucepan, melt the vegan butter over medium-high heat.
2. Once hot, sauté the shallot for about 3 minutes or until tender. Then, sauté the garlic for about 1 minute until aromatic.
3. Add in the zucchini, along with the spices and continue to sauté for 6 minutes more until tender.
4. Taste and adjust the seasonings. Top with nutritional yeast and serve. Bon appétit!

Traditional Lebanese Mutabal

Servings: 6
Cooking Time: 10 Minutes
Ingredients:
- 1 pound eggplant
- 1 onion, chopped
- 1 tablespoon garlic paste
- 4 tablespoons tahini
- 1 tablespoon coconut oil
- 2 tablespoons lemon juice
- 1/2 teaspoon ground coriander
- 1/4 cup ground cloves
- 1 teaspoon red pepper flakes
- 1 teaspoon smoked peppers
- Sea salt and ground black pepper, to taste

Directions:
1. Roast the eggplant until the skin turns black; peel the eggplant and transfer it to the bowl of your food processor.
2. Add in the remaining ingredients. Blend until everything is well incorporated.
3. Serve with crostini or pita bread, if desired. Bon appétit!

Grilled Tofu Mayo Sandwiches

Servings:2
Cooking Time:15 Minutes
Ingredients:
- ¼ cup tofu mayonnaise
- 2 slices whole-grain bread
- ¼ cucumber, sliced
- ½ cup lettuce, chopped
- ½ tomato, sliced
- 1 tsp olive oil, divided

Directions:
1. Spread the vegan mayonnaise over a bread slice, top with the cucumber, lettuce, and tomato and finish with the other slice. Heat the oil in a skillet over medium heat. Place the sandwich and grill for 3 minutes, then flip over and cook for a further 3 minutes. Cut the sandwich in half and serve.

Carrot Nori Rolls

Servings:4
Cooking Time:15 Minutes
Ingredients:
- 2 tbsp almond butter
- 2 tbsp tamari
- 4 standard nori sheets
- 1 green bell pepper, sliced
- 1 tbsp pickled ginger
- ½ cup grated carrots

Directions:
1. Preheat oven to 350 °F.
2. Whisk the almond butter and tamari until smooth and thick.
3. Place a nori sheet on a flat surface with the rough side facing up. Spoon a bit of the tamari mixture at the other side of the nori sheet, and spread on all sides. Put bell pepper slices, carrots, and ginger in a layer at the other end of the sheet. Fold up in the tahini direction to seal. Repeat the process with the remaining sheets. Arrange on a baking tray and bake for about 10 minutes until browned and crispy. Allow cooling for a few minutes before slicing into 4 pieces.

Sweet Mashed Carrots

Servings: 4
Cooking Time: 25 Minutes
Ingredients:
- 1 ½ pounds carrots, trimmed
- 3 tablespoons vegan butter
- 1 cup scallions, sliced
- 1 tablespoon maple syrup
- 1/2 teaspoon garlic powder
- 1/2 teaspoon ground allspice
- Sea salt, to taste
- 1/2 cup soy sauce
- 2 tablespoons fresh cilantro, chopped

Directions:
1. Steam the carrots for about 15 minutes until they are very tender; drain well.
2. In a sauté pan, melt the butter until sizzling. Now, turn the heat down to maintain an insistent sizzle.
3. Now, cook the scallions until they've softened. Add in the maple syrup, garlic powder, ground allspice, salt and soy sauce for about 10 minutes or until they are caramelized.
4. Add the caramelized scallions to your food processor; add in the carrots and puree the ingredients until everything is well blended.
5. Serve garnished with the fresh cilantro. Enjoy!

Bell Pepper Boats With Mango Salsa

Servings: 4
Cooking Time: 5 Minutes
Ingredients:
- 1 mango, peeled, pitted, cubed
- 1 small shallot, chopped
- 2 tablespoons fresh cilantro, minced
- 1 red chile pepper, seeded and chopped
- 1 tablespoon fresh lime juice
- 4 bell peppers, seeded and halved

Directions:
1. Thoroughly combine the mango, shallot, cilantro, red chile pepper and lime juice.
2. Spoon the mixture into the pepper halves and serve immediately.
3. Bon appétit!

Spicy Nut Burgers

Servings:4
Cooking Time:20 Minutes
Ingredients:

- ¾ cup chopped walnuts
- ¾ cup chopped cashews
- 1 medium carrot, grated
- 1 small onion, chopped
- 1 garlic clove, minced
- 1 serrano pepper, minced
- ¾ cup old-fashioned oats
- ¾ cup breadcrumbs
- 2 tbsp minced fresh cilantro
- ½ tsp ground coriander
- Salt and black pepper to taste
- 2 tsp fresh lime juice
- Canola oil for frying
- 4 sandwich rolls
- Lettuce leaves for garnish

Directions:

1. Pulse walnuts, cashews, carrot, onion, garlic, serrano pepper, oats, breadcrumbs, cilantro, coriander, lime juice, salt, and pepper in a food processor until well mixed. Remove and form into 4 burgers.
2. Warm the oil in a skillet over medium heat. Cook the burgers for 5 minutes per side, until golden brown. Serve in sandwich rolls with lettuce and a dressing of your choice.

Buttery Turnip Mash

Servings: 4
Cooking Time: 35 Minutes
Ingredients:

- 2 cups water
- 1 ½ pounds turnips, peeled and cut into small pieces
- 4 tablespoons vegan butter
- 1 cup oat milk
- 2 fresh rosemary sprigs, chopped
- 1 tablespoon fresh parsley, chopped
- 1 teaspoon ginger-garlic paste
- Kosher salt and freshly ground black pepper
- 1 teaspoon red pepper flakes, crushed

Directions:

1. Bring the water to a boil; turn the heat to a simmer and cook your turnip for about 30 minutes; drain.
2. Using an immersion blender, puree the turnips with the vegan butter, milk, rosemary, parsley, ginger-garlic paste, salt, black pepper, red pepper flakes, adding the cooking liquid, if necessary.
3. Bon appétit!

Soups, Stews & Salads

Spinach & Potato Soup

Servings:4
Cooking Time:55 Minutes
Ingredients:
- 2 tbsp olive oil
- 1 onion, chopped
- 2 garlic cloves, minced
- 4 cups vegetable broth
- 2 russet potatoes, cubed
- ½ tsp dried oregano
- ¼ tsp crushed red pepper
- 1 bay leaf
- Salt to taste
- 4 cups chopped spinach
- 1 cup green lentils, rinsed

Directions:
1. Warm the oil in a pot over medium heat. Place the onion and garlic and cook covered for 5 minutes. Stir in broth, potatoes, oregano, red pepper, bay leaf, lentils, and salt. Bring to a boil, then lower the heat and simmer uncovered for 30 minutes. Add in spinach and cook for another 5 minutes. Discard the bay leaf and serve immediately.

Rotini & Tomato Soup

Servings:4
Cooking Time:25 Minutes
Ingredients:
- 1 tbsp olive oil
- 1 medium onion, chopped
- 1 celery rib, minced
- 3 garlic cloves, minced
- 1 can crushed tomatoes
- 3 cups chopped fresh ripe tomatoes
- 2 tbsp tomato paste
- 3 cups vegetable broth
- 2 bay leaves
- 1 cup plain unsweetened soy milk
- ½ cup whole-wheat rotini pasta
- 2 tbsp chopped fresh basil

Directions:
1. Heat oil in a pot and sauté onion, celery, and garlic for 5 minutes. Add in tomatoes, tomato paste, broth, sugar, and bay leaves. Bring to a boil and add the rotini. Cook for 10 minutes. Discard bay leaves. Garnish with the basil and serve.

Vegetable & Black Bean Soup

Servings:4
Cooking Time:50 Minutes
Ingredients:
- 2 tbsp olive oil
- 1 onion, chopped
- 1 celery stalk, chopped
- 2 medium carrots, chopped
- 1 small green bell pepper, chopped
- 2 garlic cloves, minced
- 2 tomatoes, chopped
- 4 cups vegetable broth
- 1 can black beans
- 1 tsp dried thyme
- ¼ tsp cayenne pepper
- 1 tbsp minced cilantro

Directions:
1. Heat the oil in a pot over medium heat. Place in onion, celery, carrots, bell pepper, garlic, and tomatoes. Sauté for 5 minutes, stirring often. Stir in broth, beans, thyme, salt, and cayenne. Bring to a boil, then lower the heat and simmer for 15 minutes. Transfer the soup to a food processor and pulse until smooth. Serve in soup bowls garnished with cilantro.

Asian-style Bean Soup

Servings:4
Cooking Time:55 Minutes
Ingredients:
- 1 cup canned cannellini beans
- 2 tsp curry powder
- 2 tsp olive oil
- 1 red onion, diced
- 1 tbsp minced fresh ginger
- 2 cubed sweet potatoes
- 1 cup sliced zucchini
- Salt and black pepper to taste
- 4 cups vegetable stock
- 1 bunch spinach, chopped
- Toasted sesame seeds

Directions:
1. Mix the beans with 1 tsp of curry powder until well combined. Warm the oil in a pot over medium heat. Place the onion and ginger and cook for 5 minutes until soft. Add in sweet potatoes and cook for 10 minutes. Put in zucchini and cook for 5 minutes. Season with the remaining curry, pepper, and salt.
2. Pour in the stock and bring to a boil. Lower the heat and simmer for 25 minutes. Stir in beans and spinach. Cook until the spinach wilts and remove from the heat. Garnish with sesame seeds to serve.

Caribbean Lentil Stew

Servings:4
Cooking Time:50 Minutes
Ingredients:
- 2 tbsp olive oil
- 1 onion, chopped
- 1 carrot, sliced
- 2 garlic cloves, minced
- 1 sweet potato, chopped
- ¼ tsp crushed red pepper
- 1 cup red lentils, rinsed
- 1 can diced tomatoes
- 1 tsp hot curry powder
- 1 tsp chopped thyme
- ¼ tsp ground allspice
- Salt and black pepper to taste
- 1 cup water
- 1 can coconut milk

Directions:
1. Warm oil in a pot and sauté onion and carrot for 5 minutes, stirring occasionally until softened. Add in garlic, sweet potato, and crushed red pepper. Put in red lentils, tomatoes, curry powder, allspice, salt, and black pepper, stir to combine. Pour in water and simmer for 30 minutes until the vegetables are tender. Stir in coconut milk and simmer for 10 minutes. Serve hot topped with thyme.

Cannellini Bean Soup With Kale

Servings: 5
Cooking Time: 25 Minutes
Ingredients:
- 1 tablespoon olive oil
- 1/2 teaspoon ginger, minced
- 1/2 teaspoon cumin seeds
- 1 red onion, chopped
- 1 carrot, trimmed and chopped
- 1 parsnip, trimmed and chopped
- 2 garlic cloves, minced
- 5 cups vegetable broth
- 12 ounces Cannellini beans, drained
- 2 cups kale, torn into pieces
- Sea salt and ground black pepper, to taste

Directions:
1. In a heavy-bottomed pot, heat the olive over medium-high heat. Now, sauté the ginger and cumin for 1 minute or so.
2. Now, add in the onion, carrot and parsnip; continue sautéing an additional 3 minutes or until the vegetables are just tender.
3. Add in the garlic and continue to sauté for 1 minute or until aromatic.
4. Then, pour in the vegetable broth and bring to a boil. Immediately reduce the heat to a simmer and let it cook for 10 minutes.
5. Fold in the Cannellini beans and kale; continue to simmer until the kale wilts and everything is thoroughly heated. Season with salt and pepper to taste.
6. Ladle into individual bowls and serve hot. Bon appétit!

Turmeric Bean Soup

Servings:6
Cooking Time:50 Minutes
Ingredients:

- 3 tbsp olive oil
- 1 onion, chopped
- 2 carrots, chopped
- 1 sweet potato, chopped
- 1 yellow bell pepper, chopped
- 2 garlic cloves, minced
- 4 tomatoes, chopped
- 6 cups vegetable broth
- 1 bay leaf
- Salt to taste
- 1 tsp ground cayenne pepper
- 1 can white beans, drained
- ⅓ cup whole-wheat pasta
- ¼ tsp turmeric

Directions:

1. Heat the oil in a pot over medium heat. Place onion, carrots, sweet potato, bell pepper, and garlic. Cook for 5 minutes. Add in tomatoes, broth, bay leaf, salt, and cayenne pepper. Stir and bring to a boil. Lower the heat and simmer for 10 minutes. Put in white beans and simmer for 15 more minutes.
2. Cook the pasta in a pot with boiling salted water and turmeric for 8-10 minutes, until pasta is al dente. Strain and transfer to the soup. Discard the bay leaf. Spoon into a bowl and serve.

Chicago-style Vegetable Stew

Servings:4
Cooking Time:35 Minutes
Ingredients:

- 2 tbsp olive oils
- 3 shallots, chopped
- 1 carrot, sliced
- ½ cup dry white wine
- 3 new potatoes, cubed
- 1 red bell pepper, chopped
- 1 ½ cups vegetable broth
- 2 zucchini, sliced
- 1 yellow summer squash, sliced
- 1 lb plum tomatoes, chopped
- 2 Salt and black pepper to taste
- 3 cups fresh corn kernels
- 1 cup green beans
- ¼ cup fresh basil
- ¼ cup chopped fresh parsley

Directions:

1. Heat oil in a pot over medium heat. Place shallots and carrot and cook for 5 minutes. Pour in white wine, potatoes, bell pepper, and broth. Bring to a boil, lower the heat, and simmer for 5 minutes. Stir in zucchini, yellow squash and tomatoes. Sprinkle with salt and pepper. Simmer for 20 more minutes. Put in corn, green peas, basil, and parsley. Simmer an additional 5 minutes. Serve hot.

Traditional Ukrainian Borscht

Servings: 4
Cooking Time: 40 Minutes
Ingredients:

- 2 tablespoons sesame oil
- 1 red onion, chopped
- 2 carrots, trimmed and sliced
- 2 large beets, peeled and sliced
- 2 large potatoes, peeled and diced
- 4 cups vegetable stock
- 2 garlic cloves, minced
- 1/2 teaspoon caraway seeds
- 1/2 teaspoon celery seeds
- 1/2 teaspoon fennel seeds
- 1 pound red cabbage, shredded
- 1/2 teaspoon mixed peppercorns, freshly cracked
- Kosher salt, to taste
- 2 bay leaves
- 2 tablespoons wine vinegar

Directions:

1. In a Dutch oven, heat the sesame oil over a moderate flame. Once hot, sauté the onions until tender and translucent, about 6 minutes.
2. Add in the carrots, beets and potatoes and continue to sauté an additional 10 minutes, adding the vegetable stock periodically.
3. Next, stir in the garlic, caraway seeds, celery seeds, fennel seeds and continue sautéing for another 30 seconds.
4. Add in the cabbage, mixed peppercorns, salt and bay leaves. Add in the remaining stock and bring to boil.
5. Immediately turn the heat to a simmer and continue to cook for 20 to 23 minutes longer until the vegetables have softened.
6. Ladle into individual bowls and drizzle wine vinegar over it. Serve and enjoy!

Quinoa And Black Bean Salad

Servings: 4
Cooking Time: 15 Minutes
Ingredients:

- 2 cups water
- 1 cup quinoa, rinsed
- 16 ounces canned black beans, drained
- 2 Roma tomatoes, sliced
- 1 red onion, thinly sliced
- 1 cucumber, seeded and chopped
- 2 cloves garlic, pressed or minced
- 2 Italian peppers, seeded and sliced
- 2 tablespoons fresh parsley, chopped
- 2 tablespoons fresh cilantro, chopped
- 1/4 cup olive oil
- 1 lemon, freshly squeezed
- 1 tablespoon apple cider vinegar
- 1/2 teaspoon dried dill weed
- 1/2 teaspoon dried oregano
- Sea salt and ground black pepper, to taste

Directions:

1. Place the water and quinoa in a saucepan and bring it to a rolling boil. Immediately turn the heat to a simmer.
2. Let it simmer for about 13 minutes until the quinoa has absorbed all of the water; fluff the quinoa with a fork and let it cool completely. Then, transfer the quinoa to a salad bowl.
3. Add the remaining ingredients to the salad bowl and toss to combine well. Bon appétit!

Daikon & Sweet Potato Soup

Servings:6
Cooking Time:40 Minutes
Ingredients:

- 6 cups water
- 2 tsp olive oil
- 1 chopped onion
- 3 garlic cloves, minced
- 1 tbsp thyme
- 2 tsp paprika
- 2 cups peeled and chopped daikon
- 2 cups chopped sweet potatoes
- 2 cups peeled and chopped parsnips
- ½ tsp sea salt
- 1 cup fresh mint, chopped
- ½ avocado
- 2 tbsp balsamic vinegar
- 2 tbsp pumpkin seeds

Directions:

1. Heat the oil in a pot and place onion and garlic. Sauté for 3 minutes. Add in thyme, paprika, daikon, sweet potato, parsnips, water, and salt. Bring to a boil and cook for 30 minutes. Remove the soup to a food processor and add in balsamic vinegar; purée until smooth. Top with mint and pumpkin seeds to serve.

Fennel & Corn Chowder

Servings:4
Cooking Time:30 Minutes
Ingredients:

- 2 tbsp olive oil
- 1 onion, chopped
- 1 cup chopped fennel bulb
- 2 carrots, chopped
- 1 cup mushrooms, chopped
- ¼ cup whole-wheat flour
- 4 cups vegetable stock
- 2 cups canned corn
- 2 cups cubed red potatoes
- 1 cup almond milk
- ½ tsp chili paste
- Sea salt and black pepper to taste

Directions:

1. Heat the oil in a pot over medium heat. Place in onion, fennel, carrots, and mushrooms. Sauté for 5 minutes until tender. Stir in flour. Pour in vegetable stock. Lower the heat. Add in corn, potatoes, almond milk, and chili paste. Simmer for 20 minutes. Sprinkle with salt and pepper. Serve immediately.

Lime Lentil Soup

Servings:2
Cooking Time:35 Minutes
Ingredients:
- 1 tsp olive oil
- 1 onion, chopped
- 6 garlic cloves, minced
- 1 tsp chili powder
- ½ tsp ground cinnamon
- Salt to taste
- 1 cup yellow lentils
- 1 cup canned crushed tomatoes
- 2 cups water
- 1 celery stalk, chopped
- 2 cups chopped collard greens

Directions:
1. Heat oil in a pot over medium heat. Place onion and garlic and cook for 5 minutes. Stir in chili powder, celery, cinnamon, and salt. Pour in lentils, tomatoes and juices, and water. Bring to a boil, then lower the heat and simmer for 15 minutes. Stir in collard greens. Cook for an additional 5 minutes. Serve.

Roasted Wild Mushroom Soup

Servings: 3
Cooking Time: 55 Minutes
Ingredients:
- 3 tablespoons sesame oil
- 1 pound mixed wild mushrooms, sliced
- 1 white onion, chopped
- 3 cloves garlic, minced and divided
- 2 sprigs thyme, chopped
- 2 sprigs rosemary, chopped
- 1/4 cup flaxseed meal
- 1/4 cup dry white wine
- 3 cups vegetable broth
- 1/2 teaspoon red chili flakes
- Garlic salt and freshly ground black pepper, to seasoned

Directions:
1. Start by preheating your oven to 395°F.
2. Place the mushrooms in a single layer onto a parchment-lined baking pan. Drizzle the mushrooms with 1 tablespoon of the sesame oil.
3. Roast the mushrooms in the preheated oven for about 25 minutes, or until tender.
4. Heat the remaining 2 tablespoons of the sesame oil in a stockpot over medium heat. Then, sauté the onion for about 3 minutes or until tender and translucent.
5. Then, add in the garlic, thyme and rosemary and continue to sauté for 1 minute or so until aromatic. Sprinkle flaxseed meal over everything.
6. Add in the remaining ingredients and continue to simmer for 10 to 15 minutes longer or until everything is cooked through.
7. Stir in the roasted mushrooms and continue simmering for a further 12 minutes. Ladle into soup bowls and serve hot. Enjoy!

Vegetable Soup With Vermicelli

Servings:6
Cooking Time:20 Minutes
Ingredients:

- 1 tbsp olive oil 1 onion, chopped
- 4 garlic cloves, minced
- 1 can diced tomatoes
- 6 cups vegetable broth
- 8 oz vermicelli
- 1 package baby spinach

Directions:

1. Preparing the Ingredients
2. Warm the oil in a pot over medium heat. Place in onion and garlic and cook for 3 minutes. Stir in tomatoes, broth, salt, and pepper. Bring to a boil, then lower the heat and simmer for 5 minutes. Pour in vermicelli and spinach and cook for another 5 minutes. Serve warm.

Spicy Potato Soup

Servings:6
Cooking Time:25 Minutes
Ingredients:

- 3 tbsp olive oil
- 1 onion, chopped
- 1 garlic clove, minced
- 1 tbsp hot powder
- 1 lb carrots, chopped
- 2 potatoes, chopped
- 6 cups vegetable broth
- Salt to taste
- 1 can coconut milk
- 1 tbsp minced fresh parsley
- Chopped roasted cashews

Directions:

1. Heat the oil in a pot over medium heat. Place in onion and garlic and cook for 3 minutes. Add in hot powder, cook for 30 seconds. Stir in carrots, potatoes, broth, and salt. Bring to a boil, lower the heat and simmer for 15 minutes.
2. With an immersion blender, blitz the soup until smooth. Sprinkle with salt and pepper. Mix in coconut milk and cook until hot. Garnish with parsley and chopped cashews to serve.

Tofu Goulash Soup

Servings:4
Cooking Time:25 Minutes
Ingredients:

- 1 ½ cups extra-firm tofu, crumbled
- 3 tbsp plant butter
- 1 white onion
- 2 garlic cloves
- 8 oz chopped butternut squash
- 1 red bell pepper
- 1 tbsp paprika powder
- ¼ tsp red chili flakes
- 1 tbsp dried basil
- ½ tbsp crushed cardamom seeds
- Salt and black pepper to taste
- 1 ½ cups crushed tomatoes
- 4 cups vegetable broth
- 1 ½ tsp red wine vinegar
- Chopped cilantro to serve

Directions:

1. Melt plant butter in a pot over medium heat and sauté onion and garlic for 3 minutes. Stir in tofu and cook for 3 minutes; add the butternut squash, bell pepper, paprika, red chili flakes, basil, cardamom seeds, salt, and pepper. Cook for 2 minutes. Pour in tomatoes and vegetable broth. Bring to a boil, reduce the heat and simmer for 10 minutes. Mix in red wine vinegar. Garnish with cilantro and serve.

Rosemary Tomato Soup With Parmesan Croutons

Servings:6
Cooking Time:1 Hour 25 Minutes
Ingredients:

- 3 tbsp flax seed powder
- 1 ¼ cups almond flour
- 2 tsp baking powder
- 5 tbsp psyllium husk powder
- 2 tsp plain vinegar
- 3 oz plant butter
- 2 oz grated plant-based Parmesan
- 2 lb fresh ripe tomatoes
- 4 cloves garlic, peeled only
- 1 small white onion, diced
- 1 small red bell pepper, diced
- 3 tbsp olive oil
- 1 cup coconut cream
- ½ tsp dried rosemary
- ½ tsp dried oregano
- 2 tbsp chopped fresh basil
- Salt and black pepper to taste
- Basil leaves to garnish

Directions:

1. In a medium bowl, mix the flax seed powder with 9 tbsp of water and set aside to soak for 5 minutes. Preheat oven to 350°F and line a baking sheet with parchment paper.

2. In another bowl, combine almond flour, baking powder, psyllium husk powder, and salt. When the vegan "flax egg" is ready, mix in 1 ¼ cups boiling water and plain vinegar. Add in the flour mixture and whisk for 30 seconds. Form 8 flat pieces out of the dough. Place the flattened dough on the baking sheet while leaving enough room between each to allow rising.

3. Bake for 40 minutes. Remove the croutons to cool and break them into halves. Mix the plant butter with plant-based Parmesan cheese and spread the mixture in the inner parts of the croutons. Increase the oven's temperature to 450°F and bake the croutons further for 5 minutes or until golden brown and crispier.

4. In a baking pan, add tomatoes, garlic, onion, red bell pepper, and drizzle with olive oil. Roast in the oven for 25 minutes and after broil for 3 to 4 minutes until some of the tomatoes are slightly charred. Transfer to a blender and add coconut cream, rosemary, oregano, basil, salt, and black pepper. Puree until smooth and creamy. Pour the soup into serving bowls, drop some croutons on top, garnish with basil leaves, and serve.

Hearty Winter Quinoa Soup

Servings: 4
Cooking Time: 25 Minutes
Ingredients:

- 2 tablespoons olive oil
- 1 onion, chopped
- 2 carrots, peeled and chopped
- 1 parsnip, chopped
- 1 celery stalk, chopped
- 1 cup yellow squash, chopped
- 4 garlic cloves, pressed or minced
- 4 cups roasted vegetable broth
- 2 medium tomatoes, crushed
- 1 cup quinoa
- Sea salt and ground black pepper, to taste
- 1 bay laurel
- 2 cup Swiss chard, tough ribs removed and torn into pieces
- 2 tablespoons Italian parsley, chopped

Directions:

1. In a heavy-bottomed pot, heat the olive over medium-high heat. Now, sauté the onion, carrot, parsnip, celery and yellow squash for about 3 minutes or until the vegetables are just tender.

2. Add in the garlic and continue to sauté for 1 minute or until aromatic.

3. Then, stir in the vegetable broth, tomatoes, quinoa, salt, pepper and bay laurel; bring to a boil. Immediately reduce the heat to a simmer and let it cook for 13 minutes.

4. Fold in the Swiss chard; continue to simmer until the chard wilts.

5. Ladle into individual bowls and serve garnished with the fresh parsley. Bon appétit!

Indian Chana Chaat Salad

Servings: 4
Cooking Time: 45 Minutes
Ingredients:
- 1 pound dry chickpeas, soaked overnight
- 2 San Marzano tomatoes, diced
- 1 Persian cucumber, sliced
- 1 onion, chopped
- 1 bell pepper, seeded and thinly sliced
- 1 green chili, seeded and thinly sliced
- 2 handfuls baby spinach
- 1/2 teaspoon Kashmiri chili powder
- 4 curry leaves, chopped
- 1 tablespoon chaat masala
- 2 tablespoons fresh lemon juice, or to taste
- 4 tablespoons olive oil
- 1 teaspoon agave syrup
- 1/2 teaspoon mustard seeds
- 1/2 teaspoon coriander seeds
- 2 tablespoons sesame seeds, lightly toasted
- 2 tablespoons fresh cilantro, roughly chopped

Directions:
1. Drain the chickpeas and transfer them to a large saucepan. Cover the chickpeas with water by 2 inches and bring it to a boil.
2. Immediately turn the heat to a simmer and continue to cook for approximately 40 minutes.
3. Toss the chickpeas with the tomatoes, cucumber, onion, peppers, spinach, chili powder, curry leaves and chaat masala.
4. In a small mixing dish, thoroughly combine the lemon juice, olive oil, agave syrup, mustard seeds and coriander seeds.
5. Garnish with sesame seeds and fresh cilantro. Bon appétit!

Green Bean & Rice Soup

Servings:4
Cooking Time:50 Minutes
Ingredients:
- 2 tbsp olive oil
- 1 medium onion, minced
- 2 garlic cloves minced
- ½ cup brown rice
- 1 cup green beans, chopped
- 2 tbsp chopped parsley

Directions:
1. Heat oil in a pot over medium heat. Place in onion and garlic and sauté for 3 minutes. Add in rice, 4 cups water, salt, and pepper. Bring to a boil, lower the heat, and simmer for 15 minutes. Stir in beans and cook for 10 minutes. Top with parsley.

Greek-style Pinto Bean And Tomato Soup

Servings: 4
Cooking Time: 30 Minutes
Ingredients:

- 2 tablespoons olive oil
- 1 carrot, chopped
- 1 parsnip, chopped
- 1 red onion, chopped
- 1 chili pepper, minced
- 2 garlic cloves, minced
- 3 cups vegetable broth
- 1 cup canned tomatoes, crushed
- 1/2 teaspoon cumin
- Sea salt and ground black pepper, to taste
- 1 teaspoon cayenne pepper
- 1 teaspoon Greek herb mix
- 20 ounces canned pinto beans
- 12 ounces canned corn, drained
- 2 tablespoons fresh cilantro, chopped
- 2 tablespoons fresh parsley, chopped
- 2 tablespoons Kalamata olives, pitted and sliced

Directions:

1. In a heavy-bottomed pot, heat the olive over medium-high heat. Now, sauté the carrot, parsnip and onion for approximately 3 minutes or until the vegetables are just tender.
2. Add in the chili pepper and garlic and continue to sauté for 1 minute or until aromatic.
3. Then, add in the vegetable broth, canned tomatoes, cumin, salt, black pepper, cayenne pepper and Greek herb mix and bring to a boil. Immediately reduce the heat to a simmer and let it cook for 10 minutes.
4. Fold in the beans and corn and continue simmering for about 10 minutes longer until everything is thoroughly heated. Taste and adjust the seasonings.
5. Ladle into individual bowls and garnish with cilantro, parsley and olives. Bon appétit!

Spinach Soup With Gnocchi

Servings:4
Cooking Time:25 Minutes
Ingredients:

- 1 tsp olive oil
- 1 cup green bell peppers
- Salt and black pepper to taste
- 2 garlic cloves, minced
- 2 carrots, chopped
- 3 cups vegetable broth
- 1 cup gnocchi
- ¾ cup unsweetened non-dairy milk
- ¼ cup nutritional yeast
- 2 cups chopped fresh spinach
- ¼ cup pitted black olives, chopped
- Croutons, for topping

Directions:

1. Heat the oil in a pot over medium heat. Place in bell peppers, garlic, carrots, and salt and cook for 5 minutes. Stir in broth. Bring to a boil. Put in gnocchi, cook for 10 minutes. Add in spinach and cook for another 5 minutes. Stir in milk, nutritional yeast, and olives. Serve topped with croutons.

Italian Nonna's Pizza Salad

Servings: 4
Cooking Time: 15 Minutes
Ingredients:

- 1 pound macaroni
- 1 cup marinated mushrooms, sliced
- 1 cup grape tomatoes, halved
- 4 tablespoons scallions, chopped
- 1 teaspoon garlic, minced
- 1 Italian pepper, sliced
- 1/4 cup extra-virgin olive oil
- 1/4 cup balsamic vinegar
- 1 teaspoon dried oregano
- 1 teaspoon dried basil
- 1/2 teaspoon dried rosemary
- Sea salt and cayenne pepper, to taste
- 1/2 cup black olives, sliced

Directions:

1. Cook the pasta according to the package directions. Drain and rinse the pasta. Let it cool completely and then, transfer it to a salad bowl.
2. Then, add in the remaining ingredients and toss until the macaroni are well coated.
3. Taste and adjust the seasonings; place the pizza salad in your refrigerator until ready to use. Bon appétit!

Roasted Basil & Tomato Soup

Servings:4
Cooking Time:60 Minutes
Ingredients:

- 2 lb tomatoes, halved
- 2 tsp garlic powder
- 3 tbsp olive oil
- 1 tbsp balsamic vinegar
- Salt and black pepper to taste
- 4 shallots, chopped
- 2 cups vegetable broth
- ½ cup basil leaves, chopped

Directions:

1. Preheat oven to 450°F.
2. In a bowl, mix tomatoes, garlic, 2 tbsp of oil, vinegar, salt, and pepper. Arrange the tomatoes onto a baking dish. Sprinkle with some olive oil, garlic powder, balsamic vinegar, salt, and pepper. Bake for 30 minutes until the tomatoes get dark brown color. Take out from the oven; reserve.
3. Heat the remaining oil in a pot over medium heat. Place the shallots and cook for 3 minutes, stirring often. Add in roasted tomatoes and broth. Bring to a boil, then lower the heat and simmer for 10 minutes. Transfer to a food processor and blitz the soup until smooth. Serve topped with basil.

Garlicky Broccoli Soup

Servings:6
Cooking Time:35 Minutes
Ingredients:
- 2 tbsp olive oil
- 3 spring onions, chopped
- 6 cups vegetable broth
- 3 potatoes, chopped
- 2 cups broccoli florets, chopped
- 2 garlic cloves, minced
- 1 cup plain unsweetened soy milk
- Salt and black pepper to taste
- 1 tbsp minced chives

Directions:

1. Heat the oil in a pot over medium heat. Place in spring onions and garlic and sauté for 5 minutes until translucent. Add in broth, potatoes, and broccoli. Bring to a boil, then lower the heat and simmer for 20 minutes. Mix in soy milk, salt, and pepper. Cook for 5 more minutes. Serve topped with chives.

Sudanese Veggie Stew

Servings:6
Cooking Time:30 Minutes
Ingredients:
- 3 potatoes, cubed
- 3 tbsp olive oil
- 2 carrots, sliced
- 4 shallots, chopped
- 2 garlic cloves, minced
- 1 tbsp ground turmeric
- 1 tsp ground ginger
- 1 ½ cups vegetable broth
- 4 cups shredded spinach

Directions:

1. Cook the potatoes in salted water over medium heat, about 15 minutes. Drain and reserve. Heat the oil in a saucepan over medium heat. Place in carrots and shallots and cook for 5 minutes. Stir in garlic, turmeric, ginger, and salt. Cook for 1 minute more. Add in cooked potatoes and broth. Bring to a boil, then lower the heat. Stir in the spinach and cook for another 3 minutes until wilted.

Creamy Rutabaga Soup

Servings: 4
Cooking Time: 35 Minutes
Ingredients:

- 2 tablespoons olive oil
- 1 onion, chopped
- 1/2 pound rutabaga, peeled and chopped
- 1/2 pound sweet potatoes, peeled and chopped
- 1/2 cup carrots, chopped
- 1/2 cup parsnip, chopped
- 1 teaspoon ginger-garlic paste
- 3 cups vegetable broth
- Salt and ground black pepper, to taste
- 1/4 teaspoon dried dill
- 1/2 teaspoon dried oregano
- 1 teaspoon dried basil
- 1 teaspoon dried parsley flakes
- 1 teaspoon paprika
- 1/2 cup raw cashews, soaked
- 1 cup water, divided
- 1 tablespoon lemon juice
- 2 tablespoons fresh cilantro, chopped

Directions:

1. In a heavy-bottomed pot, heat the olive oil over medium-high heat. Now, sauté the onion, rutabaga, sweet potatoes, carrot and parsnip for about 5 minutes, stirring periodically.

2. Add in the ginger-garlic paste and continue sautéing for 1 minute or until fragrant.

3. Then, stir in the vegetable broth, salt, black pepper, dried dill, oregano, basil, parsley and paprika; bring to a boil. Immediately reduce the heat to a simmer and let it cook for about 20 to 22 minutes.

4. Puree the soup using an immersion blender until creamy and uniform.

5. Drain the cashews and add them to the bowl of your blender or food processor; add in the water, lemon juice and salt to taste. Blend into a cream.

6. Return the pureed mixture to the pot. Fold in the cashew cream and continue simmering until heated through or about 5 minutes longer.

7. Ladle into serving bowls and serve garnished with the fresh cilantro. Bon appétit!

Italian Penne Pasta Salad

Servings: 3
Cooking Time: 15 Minutes
Ingredients:

- 9 ounces penne pasta
- 9 ounces canned Cannellini bean, drained
- 1 small onion, thinly sliced
- 1/3 cup Niçoise olives, pitted and sliced
- 2 Italian peppers, sliced
- 1 cup cherry tomatoes, halved
- 3 cups arugula
- Dressing:
- 3 tablespoons extra-virgin olive oil
- 1 teaspoon lemon zest
- 1 teaspoon garlic, minced
- 3 tablespoons balsamic vinegar
- 1 teaspoon Italian herb mix
- Sea salt and ground black pepper, to taste

Directions:

1. Cook the penne pasta according to the package directions. Drain and rinse the pasta. Let it cool completely and then, transfer it to a salad bowl.
2. Then, add the beans, onion, olives, peppers, tomatoes and arugula to the salad bowl.
3. Mix all the dressing ingredients until everything is well incorporated. Dress your salad and serve well-chilled. Bon appétit!

Celery & Potato Soup

Servings:6
Cooking Time:55 Minutes
Ingredients:

- 2 tbsp olive oil
- 1 onion, chopped
- 1 carrot, chopped
- 1 celery stalk, chopped
- 2 garlic cloves, minced
- 1 golden beet, peeled and diced
- 1 yellow bell pepper, chopped
- 1 Yukon Gold potato, diced
- 6 cups vegetable broth
- 1 tsp dried thyme
- Salt and black pepper to taste
- 1 tbsp lemon juice

Directions:

1. Heat the oil in a pot over medium heat. Place the onion, carrot, celery, and garlic. Cook for 5 minutes or until softened. Stir in beet, bell pepper, and potato, cook uncovered for 1 minute. Pour in the broth and thyme. Season with salt and pepper. Cook for 45 minutes until the vegetables are tender. Serve sprinkled with lemon juice.

Legumes, Rice & Grains

Chickpea Garden Vegetable Medley

Servings: 4
Cooking Time: 30 Minutes
Ingredients:

- 2 tablespoons olive oil
- 1 onion, finely chopped
- 1 bell pepper, chopped
- 1 fennel bulb, chopped
- 3 cloves garlic, minced
- 2 ripe tomatoes, pureed
- 2 tablespoons fresh parsley, roughly chopped
- 2 tablespoons fresh basil, roughly chopped
- 2 tablespoons fresh coriander, roughly chopped
- 2 cups vegetable broth
- 14 ounces canned chickpeas, drained
- Kosher salt and ground black pepper, to taste
- 1/2 teaspoon cayenne pepper
- 1 teaspoon paprika
- 1 avocado, peeled and sliced

Directions:

1. In a heavy-bottomed pot, heat the olive oil over medium heat. Once hot, sauté the onion, bell pepper and fennel bulb for about 4 minutes.
2. Sauté the garlic for about 1 minute or until aromatic.
3. Add in the tomatoes, fresh herbs, broth, chickpeas, salt, black pepper, cayenne pepper and paprika. Let it simmer, stirring occasionally, for about 20 minutes or until cooked through.
4. Taste and adjust the seasonings. Serve garnished with the slices of the fresh avocado. Bon appétit!

Beluga Lentil Salad With Herbs

Servings: 4
Cooking Time: 20 Minutes
Ingredients:

- 1 cup red lentils
- 3 cups water
- 1 cup grape tomatoes, halved
- 1 green bell pepper, seeded and diced
- 1 red bell pepper, seeded and diced
- 1 red chili pepper, seeded and diced
- 1 cucumber, sliced
- 4 tablespoons shallots, chopped
- 2 tablespoons fresh parsley, roughly chopped
- 2 tablespoons fresh cilantro, roughly chopped
- 2 tablespoons fresh chives, roughly chopped
- 2 tablespoons fresh basil, roughly chopped
- 1/4 cup olive oil
- 1/2 teaspoon cumin seeds
- 1/2 teaspoon ginger, minced
- 1/2 teaspoon garlic, minced
- 1 teaspoon agave syrup
- 2 tablespoons fresh lemon juice
- 1 teaspoon lemon zest
- Sea salt and ground black pepper, to taste
- 2 ounces black olives, pitted and halved

Directions:

1. Add the brown lentils and water to a saucepan and bring to a boil over high heat. Then, turn the heat to a simmer and continue to cook for 20 minutes or until tender.
2. Place the lentils in a salad bowl.
3. Add in the vegetables and herbs and toss to combine well. In a mixing bowl, whisk the oil, cumin seeds, ginger, garlic, agave syrup, lemon juice, lemon zest, salt and black pepper.
4. Dress your salad, garnish with olives and serve at room temperature. Bon appétit!

Mediterranean-style Rice

Servings: 4
Cooking Time: 20 Minutes
Ingredients:
- 3 tablespoons vegan butter, at room temperature
- 4 tablespoons scallions, chopped
- 2 cloves garlic, minced
- 1 bay leaf
- 1 thyme sprig, chopped
- 1 rosemary sprig, chopped
- 1 ½ cups white rice
- 2 cups vegetable broth
- 1 large tomato, pureed
- Sea salt and ground black pepper, to taste
- 2 ounces Kalamata olives, pitted and sliced

Directions:
1. In a saucepan, melt the vegan butter over a moderately high flame. Cook the scallions for about 2 minutes or until tender.
2. Add in the garlic, bay leaf, thyme and rosemary and continue to sauté for about 1 minute or until aromatic.
3. Add in the rice, broth and pureed tomato. Bring to a boil; immediately turn the heat to a gentle simmer.
4. Cook for about 15 minutes or until all the liquid has absorbed. Fluff the rice with a fork, season with salt and pepper and garnish with olives; serve immediately.
5. Bon appétit!

Teff Salad With Avocado And Beans

Servings: 2
Cooking Time: 20 Minutes
Ingredients:
- 2 cups water
- 1/2 cup teff grain
- 1 teaspoon fresh lemon juice
- 3 tablespoons vegan mayonnaise
- 1 teaspoon deli mustard
- 1 small avocado, pitted, peeled and sliced
- 1 small red onion, thinly sliced
- 1 small Persian cucumber, sliced
- 1/2 cup canned kidney beans, drained
- 2 cups baby spinach

Directions:
1. In a deep saucepan, bring the water to a boil over high heat. Add in the teff grain and turn the heat to a simmer.
2. Continue to cook, covered, for about 20 minutes or until tender. Let it cool completely.
3. Add in the remaining ingredients and toss to combine. Serve at room temperature. Bon appétit!

Red Kidney Bean Patties

Servings: 4
Cooking Time: 15 Minutes
Ingredients:

- 12 ounces canned or boiled red kidney beans, drained
- 1/3 cup old-fashioned oats
- 1/4 cup all-purpose flour
- 1 teaspoon baking powder
- 1 small shallot, chopped
- 2 cloves garlic, minced
- Sea salt and ground black pepper, to taste
- 1 teaspoon paprika
- 1/2 teaspoon chili powder
- 1/2 teaspoon ground bay leaf
- 1/2 teaspoon ground cumin
- 1 chia egg
- 4 tablespoon olive oil

Directions:

1. Place the beans in a mixing bowl and mash them with a fork.
2. Thoroughly combine the beans, oats, flour, baking powder, shallot, garlic, salt, black pepper, paprika, chili powder, ground bay leaf, cumin and chia egg.
3. Shape the mixture into four patties.
4. Then, heat the olive oil in a frying pan over a moderately high heat. Fry the patties for about 8 minutes, turning them over once or twice.
5. Serve with your favorite toppings. Bon appétit!

Chickpea Stuffed Avocados

Servings: 4
Cooking Time: 10 Minutes
Ingredients:

- 2 avocados, pitted and sliced in half
- 1/2 lemon, freshly squeezed
- 4 tablespoons scallions, chopped
- 1 garlic clove, minced
- 1 medium tomato, chopped
- 1 bell pepper, seeded and chopped
- 1 red chili pepper, seeded and chopped
- 2 ounces chickpeas, boiled or cabbed, drained
- Kosher salt and ground black pepper, to taste

Directions:

1. Place your avocados on a serving platter. Drizzle the lemon juice over each avocado.
2. In a mixing bowl, gently stir the remaining ingredients for the stuffing until well incorporated.
3. Fill the avocados with the prepared mixture and serve immediately. Bon appétit!

Authentic African Mielie-meal

Servings: 4
Cooking Time: 15 Minutes
Ingredients:
- 3 cups water
- 1 cup coconut milk
- 1 cup maize meal
- 1/3 teaspoon kosher salt
- 1/4 teaspoon grated nutmeg
- 1/4 teaspoon ground cloves
- 4 tablespoons maple syrup

Directions:
1. In a saucepan, bring the water and milk to a boil; then, gradually add in the maize meal and turn the heat to a simmer.
2. Add in the salt, nutmeg and cloves. Let it cook for 10 minutes.
3. Add in the maple syrup and gently stir to combine. Bon appétit!

One-pot Italian Rice With Broccoli

Servings: 4
Cooking Time: 30 Minutes
Ingredients:
- 2 tablespoons olive oil
- 1 shallot, chopped
- 1 teaspoon ginger, minced
- 1 teaspoon garlic, minced
- 1/2 pound broccoli florets
- 1 cup Arborio rice
- 4 cups roasted vegetable broth

Directions:
1. In a medium-sized pot, heat the olive oil over a moderately high flame. Add in the shallot and cook for about 3 minutes or until tender and translucent.
2. Then, add in the ginger and garlic and continue to cook for 30 seconds more. Add in the broccoli and rice and continue to cook for 4 minutes more.
3. Pour the vegetable broth into the saucepan and bring to a boil; immediately turn the heat to a gentle simmer.
4. Cook for about 20 minutes or until all the liquid has absorbed. Taste and adjust the seasonings. Bon appétit!

Hot Bean Dipping Sauce

Servings: 10
Cooking Time: 30 Minutes
Ingredients:
- 2 cans Great Northern beans, drained
- 2 tablespoons olive oil
- 2 tablespoons Sriracha sauce
- 2 tablespoons nutritional yeast
- 4 ounces vegan cream cheese
- 1/2 teaspoon paprika
- 1/2 teaspoon cayenne pepper
- 1/2 teaspoon ground cumin
- Sea salt and ground black pepper, to taste
- 4 ounces tortilla chips

Directions:
1. Start by preheating your oven to 360°F.
2. Pulse all the ingredients, except for the tortilla chips, in your food processor until your desired consistency is reached.
3. Bake your dip in the preheated oven for about 25 minutes or until hot.
4. Serve with tortilla chips and enjoy!

Millet Salad With Pine Nuts

Servings: 4
Cooking Time: 20 Minutes
Ingredients:

- 2 ½ cups vegetable broth
- 1 cup millet
- 1 carrot, grated
- 1 tomato, diced
- 1 cucumber, diced
- 1 onion, sliced thinly
- 1/4 cup extra-virgin olive oil
- Sea salt and ground black pepper, to taste
- 1/2 cup pine nuts, chopped
- 2 tablespoons fresh cilantro, chopped

Directions:

1. Place the vegetable broth and millet in a saucepan; bring to a boil over medium-high heat.
2. Turn the heat to a simmer and let it cook for about 20 minutes; fluff the millet with a fork and let it cool completely.
3. Toss the millet with the other ingredients; toss to combine well. Bon appétit!

Everyday Savory Grits

Servings: 4
Cooking Time: 35 Minutes
Ingredients:

- 2 tablespoons vegan butter
- 1 sweet onion, chopped
- 1 teaspoon garlic, minced
- 4 cups water
- 1 cup stone-ground grits
- Sea salt and cayenne pepper, to taste

Directions:

1. In a saucepan, melt the vegan butter over medium-high heat. Once hot, cook the onion for about 3 minutes or until tender.
2. Add in the garlic and continue to sauté for 30 seconds more or until aromatic; reserve.
3. Bring the water to a boil over a moderately high heat. Stir in the grits, salt and pepper. Turn the heat to a simmer, cover and continue to cook, for about 30 minutes or until cooked through.
4. Stir in the sautéed mixture and serve warm. Bon appétit!

Colorful Spelt Salad

Servings: 4
Cooking Time: 50 Minutes
Ingredients:

- 3 ½ cups water
- 1 cup dry spelt
- 1 cup canned kidney beans, drained
- 1 bell pepper, seeded and diced
- 2 medium tomatoes, diced
- 2 tablespoons basil, chopped
- 2 tablespoons parsley, chopped
- 2 tablespoons mint, chopped
- 1/4 cup extra-virgin olive oil
- 1 teaspoon deli mustard
- 1 tablespoon fresh lime juice
- 1 tablespoon white vinegar
- Sea salt and cayenne pepper, to taste

Directions:

1. Bring the water to a boil over medium-high heat. Now, add in the spelt, turn the heat to a simmer and continue to cook for approximately 50 minutes, until the spelt is tender. Drain and allow it to cool completely.
2. Toss the spelt with the remaining ingredients; toss to combine well and place the salad in your refrigerator until ready to serve.
3. Bon appétit!

Easy Sweet Maize Meal Porridge

Servings: 2
Cooking Time: 15 Minutes
Ingredients:

- 2 cups water
- 1/2 cup maize meal
- 1/4 teaspoon ground allspice
- 1/4 teaspoon salt
- 2 tablespoons brown sugar
- 2 tablespoons almond butter

Directions:

1. In a saucepan, bring the water to a boil; then, gradually add in the maize meal and turn the heat to a simmer.
2. Add in the ground allspice and salt. Let it cook for 10 minutes.
3. Add in the brown sugar and almond butter and gently stir to combine. Bon appétit!

Powerful Teff Bowl With Tahini Sauce

Servings: 4
Cooking Time: 20 Minutes
Ingredients:

- 3 cups water
- 1 cup teff
- 2 garlic cloves, pressed
- 4 tablespoons tahini
- 2 tablespoons tamari sauce
- 2 tablespoons white vinegar
- 1 teaspoon agave nectar
- 1 teaspoon deli mustard
- 1 teaspoon Italian herb mix
- 1 cup canned chickpeas, drained
- 2 cups mixed greens
- 1 cup grape tomatoes, halved
- 1 Italian peppers, seeded and diced

Directions:

1. In a deep saucepan, bring the water to a boil over high heat. Add in the teff grain and turn the heat to a simmer.
2. Continue to cook, covered, for about 20 minutes or until tender. Let it cool completely and transfer to a salad bowl.
3. In the meantime, mix the garlic, tahini, tamari sauce, vinegar, agave nectar, mustard and Italian herb mix; whisk until everything is well incorporated.
4. Add the canned chickpeas, mixed greens, tomatoes and peppers to the salad bowl; toss to combine. Dress the salad and toss again. Serve at room temperature. Bon appétit!

Split Pea And Potato Soup

Servings: 5
Cooking Time: 1 Hour 5 Minutes
Ingredients:

- 2 tablespoons olive oil
- 1 large onion, chopped
- 2 medium carrots, chopped
- 2 medium potatoes, diced
- 1 teaspoon garlic, minced
- 2 cups split peas, soaked overnight and drained
- 5 cups vegetable broth
- 2 tablespoons fresh cilantro, chopped

Directions:

1. In a Dutch oven, heat the olive oil over medium-high heat. Once hot, sauté the onion, carrot and potatoes for 4 minutes, stirring periodically to ensure even cooking.
2. Add in the garlic and continue to sauté for 30 seconds or until aromatic.
3. Add in the peas and vegetable broth. Continue to cook, partially covered, for 1 hour more or until cooked through.
4. Bon appétit!

Black Bean And Spinach Stew

Servings: 4
Cooking Time: 1 Hour 35 Minutes
Ingredients:

- 2 cups black beans, soaked overnight and drained
- 2 tablespoons olive oil
- 1 onion, peeled, halved
- 1 jalapeno pepper, sliced
- 2 peppers, seeded and sliced
- 1 cup button mushrooms, sliced
- 2 garlic cloves, chopped
- 2 cups vegetable broth
- 1 teaspoon paprika
- Kosher salt and ground black pepper, to taste
- 1 bay leaf
- 2 cups spinach, torn into pieces

Directions:

1. Cover the soaked beans with a fresh change of cold water and bring to a boil. Let it boil for about 10 minutes. Turn the heat to a simmer and continue to cook for 50 to 55 minutes or until tender.
2. In a heavy-bottomed pot, heat the olive oil over medium heat. Once hot, sauté the onion and peppers for about 3 minutes.
3. Sauté the garlic and mushrooms for approximately 3 minutes or until the mushrooms release the liquid and the garlic is fragrant.
4. Add in the vegetable broth, paprika, salt, black pepper, bay leaf and cooked beans. Let it simmer, stirring periodically, for about 25 minutes or until cooked through.
5. Afterwards, add in the spinach and let it simmer, covered, for about 5 minutes. Bon appétit!

Freekeh Salad With Za'atar

Servings: 4
Cooking Time: 35 Minutes
Ingredients:

- 1 cup freekeh
- 2 ½ cups water
- 1 cup grape tomatoes, halved
- 2 bell peppers, seeded and sliced
- 1 habanero pepper, seeded and sliced
- 1 onion, thinly sliced
- 2 tablespoons fresh cilantro, chopped
- 2 tablespoons fresh parsley, chopped
- 2 ounces green olives, pitted and sliced
- 1/4 cup extra-virgin olive oil
- 2 tablespoons lemon juice
- 1 teaspoon deli mustard
- 1 teaspoon za'atar
- Sea salt and ground black pepper, to taste

Directions:

1. Place the freekeh and water in a saucepan. Bring to a boil over medium-high heat.
2. Immediately turn the heat to a simmer for 30 to 35 minutes, stirring occasionally to promote even cooking. Let it cool completely.
3. Toss the cooked freekeh with the remaining ingredients. Toss to combine well.
4. Bon appétit!

Grandma's Pilau With Garden Vegetables

Servings: 4
Cooking Time: 45 Minutes
Ingredients:

- 2 tablespoons olive oil
- 1 onion, chopped
- 1 carrot, trimmed and grated
- 1 parsnip, trimmed and grated
- 1 celery with leaves, chopped
- 1 teaspoon garlic, chopped
- 1 cup brown rice
- 2 cups vegetable broth
- 2 tablespoons fresh parsley, chopped
- 2 tablespoons finely basil, chopped

Directions:

1. Heat the olive oil in a saucepan over medium-high heat.
2. Once hot, cook the onion, carrot, parsnip and celery for about 3 minutes until just tender. Add in the garlic and continue to sauté for 1 minute or so until aromatic.
3. In a lightly oiled casserole dish, place the rice, flowed by the sautéed vegetables and broth.
4. Bake, covered, at 375°F for about 40 minutes, stirring after 20 minutes.
5. Garnish with fresh parsley and basil and serve warm. Bon appétit!

Quick Everyday Chili

Servings: 5
Cooking Time: 35 Minutes
Ingredients:

- 2 tablespoons olive oil
- 1 large onion, chopped
- 1 celery with leaves, trimmed and diced
- 1 carrot, trimmed and diced
- 1 sweet potato, peeled and diced
- 3 cloves garlic, minced
- 1 jalapeno pepper, minced
- 1 teaspoon cayenne pepper
- 1 teaspoon coriander seeds
- 1 teaspoon fennel seeds
- 1 teaspoon paprika
- 2 cups stewed tomatoes, crushed
- 2 tablespoons tomato ketchup
- 2 teaspoons vegan bouillon granules
- 1 cup water
- 1 cup cream of onion soup
- 2 pounds canned pinto beans, drained
- 1 lime, sliced

Directions:

1. In a heavy-bottomed pot, heat the olive oil over medium heat. Once hot, sauté the onion, celery, carrot and sweet potato for about 4 minutes.
2. Sauté the garlic and jalapeno pepper for about 1 minute or so.
3. Add in the spices, tomatoes, ketchup, vegan bouillon granules, water, cream of onion soup and canned beans. Let it simmer, stirring occasionally, for about 30 minutes or until cooked through.
4. Serve garnished with the slices of lime. Bon appétit!

Sweet Cornbread Muffins

Servings: 8
Cooking Time: 30 Minutes
Ingredients:

- 1 cup all-purpose flour
- 1 cup yellow cornmeal
- 1 teaspoon baking powder
- 1 teaspoon baking soda
- 1 teaspoon kosher salt
- 1/2 cup sugar
- 1/2 teaspoon ground cinnamon
- 1 1/2 cups almond milk
- 1/2 cup vegan butter, melted
- 2 tablespoons applesauce

Directions:

1. Start by preheating your oven to 420°F. Now, spritz a muffin tin with a nonstick cooking spray.
2. In a mixing bowl, thoroughly combine the flour, cornmeal, baking soda, baking powder, salt, sugar and cinnamon.
3. Gradually add in the milk, butter and applesauce, whisking constantly to avoid lumps.
4. Scrape the batter into the prepared muffin tin. Bake your muffins for about 25 minutes or until a tester inserted in the middle comes out dry and clean.
5. Transfer them to a wire rack to rest for 5 minutes before unmolding and serving. Bon appétit!

Middle Eastern Za'atar Hummus

Servings: 8
Cooking Time: 10 Minutes
Ingredients:

- 10 ounces chickpeas, boiled and drained
- 1/4 cup tahini
- 2 tablespoons extra-virgin olive oil
- 2 tablespoons sun-dried tomatoes, chopped
- 1 lemon, freshly squeezed
- 2 garlic cloves, minced
- Kosher salt and ground black pepper, to taste
- 1/2 teaspoon smoked paprika
- 1 teaspoon Za'atar

Directions:

1. Blitz all the ingredients in your food processor until creamy and uniform.
2. Place in your refrigerator until ready to serve.
3. Bon appétit!

Bulgur Wheat Salad

Servings: 4
Cooking Time: 25 Minutes
Ingredients:

- 1 cup bulgur wheat
- 1 ½ cups vegetable broth
- 1 teaspoon sea salt
- 1 teaspoon fresh ginger, minced
- 4 tablespoons olive oil
- 1 onion, chopped
- 8 ounces canned garbanzo beans, drained
- 2 large roasted peppers, sliced
- 2 tablespoons fresh parsley, roughly chopped

Directions:

1. In a deep saucepan, bring the bulgur wheat and vegetable broth to a simmer; let it cook, covered, for 12 to 13 minutes.
2. Let it stand for about 10 minutes and fluff with a fork.
3. Add the remaining ingredients to the cooked bulgur wheat; serve at room temperature or well-chilled. Bon appétit!

Old-fashioned Chili

Servings: 4
Cooking Time: 1 Hour 30 Minutes
Ingredients:

- 3/4 pound red kidney beans, soaked overnight
- 2 tablespoons olive oil
- 1 onion, chopped
- 2 bell peppers, chopped
- 1 red chili pepper, chopped
- 2 ribs celery, chopped
- 2 cloves garlic, minced
- 2 bay leaves
- 1 teaspoon ground cumin
- 1 teaspoon thyme, chopped
- 1 teaspoon black peppercorns
- 20 ounces tomatoes, crushed
- 2 cups vegetable broth
- 1 teaspoon smoked paprika
- Sea salt, to taste
- 2 tablespoons fresh cilantro, chopped
- 1 avocado, pitted, peeled and sliced

Directions:

1. Cover the soaked beans with a fresh change of cold water and bring to a boil. Let it boil for about 10 minutes. Turn the heat to a simmer and continue to cook for 50 to 55 minutes or until tender.
2. In a heavy-bottomed pot, heat the olive oil over medium heat. Once hot, sauté the onion, bell pepper and celery.
3. Sauté the garlic, bay leaves, ground cumin, thyme and black peppercorns for about 1 minute or so.
4. Add in the diced tomatoes, vegetable broth, paprika, salt and cooked beans. Let it simmer, stirring periodically, for 25 to 30 minutes or until cooked through.
5. Serve garnished with fresh cilantro and avocado. Bon appétit!

Traditional Tuscan Bean Stew (ribollita)

Servings: 5
Cooking Time: 25 Minutes
Ingredients:

- 3 tablespoons olive oil
- 1 medium leek, chopped
- 1 celery with leaves, chopped
- 1 zucchini, diced
- 1 Italian pepper, sliced
- 3 garlic cloves, crushed
- 2 bay leaves
- Kosher salt and ground black pepper, to taste
- 1 teaspoon cayenne pepper
- 1 can tomatoes, crushed
- 2 cups vegetable broth
- 2 cans Great Northern beans, drained
- 2 cups Lacinato kale, torn into pieces
- 1 cup crostini

Directions:

1. In a heavy-bottomed pot, heat the olive oil over medium heat. Once hot, sauté the leek, celery, zucchini and pepper for about 4 minutes.
2. Sauté the garlic and bay leaves for about 1 minute or so.
3. Add in the spices, tomatoes, broth and canned beans. Let it simmer, stirring occasionally, for about 15 minutes or until cooked through.
4. Add in the Lacinato kale and continue simmering, stirring occasionally, for 4 minutes.
5. Serve garnished with crostini. Bon appétit!

Overnight Oatmeal With Prunes

Servings: 2
Cooking Time: 5 Minutes
Ingredients:

- 1 cup hemp milk
- 1 tablespoon flax seed, ground
- 2/3 cup rolled oats
- 2 ounces prunes, sliced
- 2 tablespoons agave syrup
- A pinch of salt
- 1/2 teaspoon ground cinnamon

Directions:

1. Divide the ingredients, except for the prunes, between two mason jars.
2. Cover and shake to combine well. Let them sit overnight in your refrigerator.
3. Garnish with sliced prunes just before serving. Enjoy!

Polenta With Mushrooms And Chickpeas

Servings: 4
Cooking Time: 25 Minutes
Ingredients:

- 3 cups vegetable broth
- 1 cup yellow cornmeal
- 2 tablespoons olive oil
- 1 onion, chopped
- 1 bell pepper, seeded and sliced
- 1 pound Cremini mushrooms, sliced
- 2 garlic cloves, minced
- 1/2 cup dry white wine
- 1/2 cup vegetable broth
- Kosher salt and freshly ground black pepper, to taste
- 1 teaspoon paprika
- 1 cup canned chickpeas, drained

Directions:

1. In a medium saucepan, bring the vegetable broth to a boil over medium-high heat. Now, add in the cornmeal, whisking continuously to prevent lumps.
2. Reduce the heat to a simmer. Continue to simmer, whisking periodically, for about 18 minutes, until the mixture has thickened.
3. Meanwhile, heat the olive oil in a saucepan over a moderately high heat. Cook the onion and pepper for about 3 minutes or until just tender and fragrant.
4. Add in the mushrooms and garlic; continue to sauté, gradually adding the wine and broth, for 4 more minutes or until cooked through. Season with salt, black pepper and paprika. Stir in the chickpeas.
5. Spoon the mushroom mixture over your polenta and serve warm. Bon appétit!

Spiced Roasted Chickpeas

Servings: 6
Cooking Time: 25 Minutes
Ingredients:
- 2 cups canned chickpeas, drained
- 2 tablespoons olive oil
- Sea salt and red pepper, to taste
- 1 teaspoon chili powder
- 1/2 teaspoon curry powder
- 1/2 teaspoon garlic powder

Directions:
1. Pat the chickpeas dry using paper towels. Drizzle olive oil over the chickpeas.
2. Roast the chickpeas in the preheated oven at 400°F for about 25 minutes, tossing them once or twice.
3. Toss your chickpeas with the spices and enjoy!

Traditional Mnazaleh Stew

Servings: 4
Cooking Time: 25 Minutes
Ingredients:
- 4 tablespoons olive oil
- 1 onion, chopped
- 1 large-sized eggplant, peeled and diced
- 1 cup carrots, chopped
- 2 garlic cloves, minced
- 2 large-sized tomatoes, pureed
- 1 teaspoon Baharat seasoning
- 2 cups vegetable broth
- 14 ounces canned chickpeas, drained
- Kosher salt and ground black pepper, to taste
- 1 medium-sized avocado, pitted, peeled and sliced

Directions:
1. In a heavy-bottomed pot, heat the olive oil over medium heat. Once hot, sauté the onion, eggplant and carrots for about 4 minutes.
2. Sauté the garlic for about 1 minute or until aromatic.
3. Add in the tomatoes, Baharat seasoning, broth and canned chickpeas. Let it simmer, stirring occasionally, for about 20 minutes or until cooked through.
4. Season with salt and pepper. Serve garnished with slices of the fresh avocado. Bon appétit!

Italian Bean Salad

Servings: 4
Cooking Time: 1 Hour
Ingredients:

- 3/4 pound cannellini beans, soaked overnight and drained
- 2 cups cauliflower florets
- 1 red onion, thinly sliced
- 1 teaspoon garlic, minced
- 1/2 teaspoon ginger, minced
- 1 jalapeno pepper, minced
- 1 cup grape tomatoes, quartered
- 1/3 cup extra-virgin olive oil
- 1 tablespoon lime juice
- 1 teaspoon Dijon mustard
- 1/4 cup white vinegar
- 2 cloves garlic, pressed
- 1 teaspoon Italian herb mix
- Kosher salt and ground black pepper, to season
- 2 ounces green olives, pitted and sliced

Directions:

1. Cover the soaked beans with a fresh change of cold water and bring to a boil. Let it boil for about 10 minutes. Turn the heat to a simmer and continue to cook for 60 minutes or until tender.
2. Meanwhile, boil the cauliflower florets for about 6 minutes or until just tender.
3. Allow your beans and cauliflower to cool completely; then, transfer them to a salad bowl.
4. Add in the remaining ingredients and toss to combine well. Taste and adjust the seasonings.
5. Bon appétit!

Chinese-style Soybean Salad

Servings: 4
Cooking Time: 10 Minutes
Ingredients:

- 1 can soybeans, drained
- 1 cup arugula
- 1 cup baby spinach
- 1 cup green cabbage, shredded
- 1 onion, thinly sliced
- 1/2 teaspoon garlic, minced
- 1 teaspoon ginger, minced
- 1/2 teaspoon deli mustard
- 2 tablespoons soy sauce
- 1 tablespoon rice vinegar
- 1 tablespoon lime juice
- 2 tablespoons tahini
- 1 teaspoon agave syrup

Directions:

1. In a salad bowl, place the soybeans, arugula, spinach, cabbage and onion; toss to combine.
2. In a small mixing dish, whisk the remaining ingredients for the dressing.
3. Dress your salad and serve immediately. Bon appétit!

Other Favorites

Chocolate Walnut Spread

Servings: 15
Cooking Time: 20 Minutes
Ingredients:

- 1 cup walnuts
- 1 teaspoon pure vanilla extract
- 1/2 cup agave nectar
- 4 tablespoons cocoa powder
- A pinch of ground cinnamon
- A pinch of grated nutmeg
- A pinch of sea salt
- 4 tablespoons almond milk

Directions:
1. Roast the walnuts in the preheated oven at 350 °F for approximately 10 minutes until they are fragrant and lightly browned.
2. In your food processor or a high-speed blender, pulse the walnuts until ground. Then, process the mixture for 5 minutes more, scraping down the sides and bottom of the bowl.
3. Add in the remaining ingredients.
4. Run your machine for a further 5 minutes or until the mixture is completely creamy and smooth. Enjoy!

Raspberry Star Anise Jelly

Servings: 20
Cooking Time: 35 Minutes
Ingredients:

- 2 pounds fresh raspberries
- 2 pounds granulated sugar
- 1 heaping teaspoon anise star
- 1 vanilla bean, split lengthwise

Directions:
1. Mix all the ingredients in a saucepan.
2. Continue to cook over medium heat, stirring constantly, until the sauce has reduced and thickened for about 25 minutes.
3. Remove from the heat. Leave your jam to sit for 10 minutes. Ladle into sterilized jars and cover with the lids. Let it cool completely.
4. Store in the cupboard for a few months. Bon appétit!

Roasted Pepper Spread

Servings: 10
Cooking Time: 10 Minutes
Ingredients:

- 2 red bell peppers, roasted and seeded
- 1 jalapeno pepper, roasted and seeded
- 4 ounces sun-dried tomatoes in oil, drained
- 2/3 cup sunflower seeds
- 2 tablespoons onion, chopped
- 1 garlic clove
- 1 tablespoon Mediterranean herb mix
- Sea salt and ground black pepper, to taste
- 1/2 teaspoon turmeric powder
- 1 teaspoon ground cumin
- 2 tablespoons tahini

Directions:
1. Place all the ingredients in the bowl of your blender or food processor.
2. Process until creamy, uniform and smooth.
3. Store in an airtight container in your refrigerator for up to 2 weeks. Bon appétit!

Basic Homemade Tahini

Servings: 16
Cooking Time: 10 Minutes
Ingredients:

- 10 ounces sesame seeds, hulled
- 3 tablespoons canola oil
- 1/4 teaspoon kosher salt

Directions:

1. Toast the sesame seeds in a nonstick skillet for about 4 minutes, stirring continuously. Cool the sesame seeds completely.
2. Transfer the sesame seeds to the bowl of your food processor. Process for about 1 minute.
3. Add in the oil and salt and process for a further 4 minutes, scraping down the bottom and sides of the bowl.
4. Store your tahini in the refrigerator for up to 1 month. Bon appétit!

Old-fashioned Sweet Potato Cakes

Servings: 5
Cooking Time: 30 Minutes
Ingredients:

- 1 ½ pounds sweet potatoes, peeled, grated and squeezed
- 1 Vidalia onion, chopped
- 2 cloves garlic, minced
- 1 cup all-purpose flour
- 1/4 cup cornstarch
- 1 teaspoon baking powder
- 2 flax eggs
- Sea salt and freshly ground black pepper, to taste
- 1 teaspoon Za'atar spice
- 1/3 cup olive oil

Directions:

1. In a mixing bowl, thoroughly combine the sweet potatoes, Vidalia onion, garlic, flour, cornstarch, baking powder, flax eggs, salt, black pepper and Za'atar spice.
2. Preheat the oil in a frying pan over a moderate heat.
3. Spoon 1/4 cup of the potato mixture into the pan and cook the potato cakes until golden brown on both sides or about 10 minutes. Repeat with the remaining batter.
4. Serve with toppings of choice. Bon appétit!

Crunchy Peanut Butter

Servings: 20
Cooking Time: 10 Minutes
Ingredients:

- 2 ½ cups peanuts
- 1/2 teaspoon coarse sea salt
- 1/2 teaspoon cinnamon powder
- 10 dates, pitted

Directions:

1. Roast the peanuts in the preheated oven at 350 °F for approximately 7 minutes until the peanuts are fragrant and lightly browned.
2. In your food processor or a high-speed blender, pulse the peanuts until ground. Reserve for about 1/2 cup of the mixture.
3. Then, process the mixture for 2 minutes more, scraping down the sides and bottom of the bowl.
4. Add in the salt, cinnamon and dates.
5. Run your machine for another 2 minutes or until your butter is smooth. Add in the reserved peanuts and stir with a spoon. Enjoy!

Pecan And Apricot Butter

Servings: 16
Cooking Time: 15 Minutes
Ingredients:

- 2 ½ cups pecans
- 1/2 cup dried apricots, chopped
- 1/2 cup sunflower oil
- 1 teaspoon bourbon vanilla
- 1/4 teaspoon ground anise
- 1/2 teaspoon cinnamon
- 1/8 teaspoon grated nutmeg
- 1/8 teaspoon salt

Directions:

1. In your food processor or a high-speed blender, pulse the pecans until ground. Then, process the pecans for 5 minutes more, scraping down the sides and bottom of the bowl.
2. Add in the remaining ingredients.
3. Run your machine for a further 5 minutes or until the mixture is completely creamy and smooth. Enjoy!

Raw Mixed Berry Jam

Servings: 10
Cooking Time: 1 Hour 5 Minutes
Ingredients:

- 1/4 pound fresh raspberries
- 1/4 pound fresh strawberries, hulled
- 1/4 pound fresh blackberries
- 2 tablespoons lemon juice, freshly squeezed
- 10 dates, pitted
- 3 tablespoons chia seeds

Directions:

1. Puree all the ingredients in your blender or food processor.
2. Let it sit for about 1 hour, stirring periodically.
3. Store your jam in sterilized jars in your refrigerator for up to 4 days. Bon appétit!

Easy Vegetable Pajeon

Servings: 4
Cooking Time: 20 Minutes
Ingredients:

- 1/2 cup all-purpose flour
- 1/2 cup potato starch
- 1 teaspoon baking powder
- 1/3 teaspoon Himalayan salt
- 1/2 cup kimchi, finely chopped
- 4 scallions, chopped
- 1 carrot, trimmed and chopped
- 2 bell peppers, chopped
- 1 green chili pepper, chopped
- 1 cup kimchi liquid
- 2 tablespoons olive oil
- Dipping sauce:
- 2 tablespoons soy sauce
- 2 teaspoons rice vinegar
- 1 teaspoon fresh ginger, finely grated

Directions:

1. Thoroughly combine the flour, potato starch, baking powder and salt. In a separate bowl, combine the vegetables and kimchi liquid.
2. Add the vegetable mixture to the dry flour mixture; stir to combine well.
3. Then, heat the oil in a frying pan over a moderate flame. Cook the Pajeon for 2 to 3 minutes per side until crispy.
4. Meanwhile, mix the sauce ingredients. Serve your Pajeon with the sauce for dipping. Bon appétit!

Healthy Chocolate Peanut Butter

Servings: 20
Cooking Time: 15 Minutes
Ingredients:

- 2 ½ cups peanuts
- 1/2 teaspoon coarse sea salt
- 1/2 teaspoon cinnamon powder
- 1/2 cup cocoa powder
- 10 dates, pitted

Directions:

1. Roast the peanuts in the preheated oven at 350°F for approximately 7 minutes until the peanuts are fragrant and lightly browned.
2. In your food processor or a high-speed blender, pulse the peanuts until ground. Then, process the mixture for 2 minutes more, scraping down the sides and bottom of the bowl.
3. Add in the salt, cinnamon, cocoa powder and dates.
4. Run your machine for another 2 minutes or until your butter is completely creamy and smooth. Enjoy!

Traditional Hanukkah Latkes

Servings: 6
Cooking Time: 30 Minutes
Ingredients:

- 1 ½ pounds potatoes, peeled, grated and drained
- 3 tablespoons green onions, sliced
- 1/3 cup all-purpose flour
- 1/2 teaspoon baking powder
- 1/2 teaspoon sea salt, preferably kala namak
- 1/4 teaspoon ground black pepper
- 1/2 olive oil
- 5 tablespoons applesauce
- 1 tablespoon fresh dill, roughly chopped

Directions:

1. Thoroughly combine the grated potato, green onion, flour, baking powder, salt and black pepper.
2. Preheat the olive oil in a frying pan over a moderate heat.
3. Spoon 1/4 cup of potato mixture into the pan and cook your latkes until golden brown on both sides. Repeat with the remaining batter.
4. Serve with applesauce and fresh dill. Bon appétit!

Cinnamon Cashew Butter

Servings: 9
Cooking Time: 15 Minutes
Ingredients:

- 2 cups raw cashew nuts
- A pinch of sea salt
- A pinch of grated nutmeg
- 1 teaspoon ground cinnamon
- 4 tablespoons agave syrup
- 2 tablespoons peanut oil

Directions:

1. Roast the cashew nuts in the preheated oven at 350 °F for approximately 8 minutes until the peanuts are fragrant and lightly browned.
2. In your food processor or a high-speed blender, pulse the cashew nuts until ground. Then, process the nuts for 2 minutes more, scraping down the sides and bottom of the bowl.
3. Add in the salt, nutmeg, cinnamon, agave syrup and oil.
4. Run your machine for another 2 minutes or until your butter is completely creamy and smooth. Enjoy!

Apple And Almond Butter Balls

Servings: 12
Cooking Time: 15 Minutes
Ingredients:
- 1/2 cup almond butter
- 1 cup apple butter
- 1/3 cup almonds
- 1 cup fresh dates, pitted
- 1/2 teaspoon ground cinnamon
- 1/4 teaspoon ground cardamom
- 1/2 teaspoon almond extract
- 1/2 teaspoon rum extract
- 2 ½ cups old-fashioned oats

Directions:
1. Place the almond butter, apple butter, almonds, dates and spices in the bowl of your blender or food processor.
2. Process the mixture until you get a thick paste.
3. Stir in the oats and pulse a few more times to blend well. Roll the mixture into balls and serve well-chilled.

Old-fashioned Pecan Spread

Servings: 16
Cooking Time: 10 Minutes
Ingredients:
- 2 cups pecan, soaked and drained
- 5 tablespoons coconut oil
- 4 tablespoons orange juice
- 1 cup dates, pitted

Directions:
1. In your food processor or a high-speed blender, pulse the pecans until ground.
2. Then, process the nuts for 2 minutes more, scraping down the sides and bottom of the bowl.
3. Add in the coconut oil, orange juice and dates. Continue to blend until your desired consistency is achieved.
4. Bon appétit!

Sweet Cinnamon Walnut Spread

Servings: 16
Cooking Time: 20 Minutes
Ingredients:
- 1 ½ cups raw walnuts
- 2 ounces dark chocolate, broken into chunks
- 1 teaspoon ground cinnamon
- A pinch of sea salt
- A pinch of grated nutmeg
- 1/3 cup agave syrup

Directions:
1. Roast the walnuts in the preheated oven at 350°F for approximately 10 minutes until they are fragrant and lightly browned.
2. In your food processor or a high-speed blender, pulse the walnuts until ground. Then, process the mixture for 5 minutes more, scraping down the sides and bottom of the bowl.
3. Add in the remaining ingredients.
4. Run your machine for a further 5 minutes or until the mixture is completely creamy and smooth. Enjoy!

Nutty Chocolate Fudge Spread

Servings: 16
Cooking Time: 25 Minutes
Ingredients:
- 1 pound walnuts
- 1 ounce coconut oil, melted
- 2 tablespoons corn flour
- 4 tablespoons cocoa powder
- A pinch of grated nutmeg
- 1/3 teaspoon ground cinnamon
- A pinch of salt

Directions:
1. Roast the walnuts in the preheated oven at 350°F for approximately 10 minutes until your walnuts are fragrant and lightly browned.
2. In your food processor or a high-speed blender, pulse the walnuts until ground. Then, process them for 5 minutes more, scraping down the sides and bottom of the bowl; reserve.
3. Melt the coconut oil over medium heat. Add in the corn flour and continue to cook until the mixture starts to boil.
4. Turn the heat to a simmer, add in the cocoa powder, nutmeg, cinnamon and salt; continue to cook, stirring occasionally, for about 10 minutes.
5. Fold in the ground walnuts, stir to combine and store in a glass jar. Enjoy!

Spiced Cauliflower Bites

Servings: 4
Cooking Time: 25 Minutes
Ingredients:
- 1 pound cauliflower florets
- 1 cup all-purpose flour
- 1 tablespoon olive oil
- 1 tablespoon tomato paste
- 1 teaspoon onion powder
- 1 teaspoon garlic powder
- 1 teaspoon smoked paprika
- 1/2 teaspoon dried oregano
- 1/2 teaspoon dried basil
- 1/4 cup hot sauce

Directions:
1. Begin by preheating your oven to 450°F. Pat the cauliflower florets dry using a kitchen towel.
2. Mix the remaining ingredients until well combined. Dip the cauliflower florets in the batter until well coated on all sides.
3. Place the cauliflower florets in a parchment-lined baking pan.
4. Roast for about 25 minutes or until cooked through. Bon appétit!

Homemade Apple Butter

Servings: 16
Cooking Time: 35 Minutes
Ingredients:

- 5 pounds apples, peeled, cored and diced
- 1 cup water
- 2/3 cup granulated brown sugar
- 1 tablespoon ground cinnamon
- 1 teaspoon ground cloves
- 1 tablespoon vanilla essence
- A pinch of freshly grated nutmeg
- A pinch of salt

Directions:

1. Add the apples and water to a heavy-bottomed pot and cook for about 20 minutes.
2. Then, mash the cooked apples with a potato masher; stir the sugar, cinnamon, cloves, vanilla, nutmeg and salt into the mashed apples; stir to combine well.
3. Continue to simmer until the butter has thickened to your desired consistency.
4. Bon appétit!

Coconut "feta" Cheese

Servings: 12
Cooking Time: 30 Minutes
Ingredients:

- 1 ½ cups full-fat coconut milk
- 1/2 cup hot water
- 1 teaspoon Himalayan salt
- 1/2 teaspoon garlic powder
- 1/4 teaspoon dried dill weed
- 1 tablespoon coconut oil
- 2 tablespoons nutritional yeast
- 4 teaspoons agar agar powder
- 1 tablespoon white vinegar

Directions:

1. In a saucepan, place the milk and water.
2. Add in the salt, garlic powder, dill, coconut oil, nutritional yeast and agar agar powder and whisk to combine well.
3. Heat the mixture over medium heat, stirring continuously; bring to a rapid boil. Add in the vinegar and stir to combine well.
4. Turn the heat to a simmer and continue to whisk for 6 to 7 minutes more or until the mixture is uniform and smooth.
5. Spoon the mixture into lightly greased molds. Let it stand for 20 minutes at room temperature. Place in your refrigerator for at least 2 hours or until set.
6. Store in your refrigerator for up to a week. Enjoy!

Delicious Lemon Butter

Servings: 8
Cooking Time: 10 Minutes
Ingredients:

- 1/2 cup granulated sugar
- 2 tablespoons cornstarch
- 1/2 teaspoon lemon zest, grated
- 1 cup water
- 2 tablespoons fresh lemon juice
- 2 tablespoons coconut oil

Directions:

1. In a saucepan, combine the sugar, cornstarch and lemon zest over a moderate heat.
2. Stir in the water and lemon juice and continue to cook until the mixture has thickened. Heat off.
3. Stir in the coconut oil. Bon appétit!

Sauces & Condiments

Red Pepper And Tomato Sauce

Servings: 6
Cooking Time: 1 Hour 20 Minutes
Ingredients:

- 1 pound red peppers
- 2 tablespoons olive oil
- 1 shallot, chopped
- 2 garlic cloves, minced
- 1 pound tomatoes, chopped
- 1/2 cup vegetable broth
- 1 teaspoon cayenne pepper
- 1 teaspoon dried basil
- 1/2 teaspoon dried oregano
- 2 tablespoons red wine
- Sea salt and freshly ground pepper, to taste

Directions:

1. Place the peppers directly over a low gas flame; roast the peppers for about 8 minutes until they are charred on all sides.
2. Let the peppers steam in a plastic bag or covered bowl for about 30 minutes. Remove the blackened skin and core and transfer the flesh to your food processor
3. Blitz until a smooth paste forms.
4. Heat the prepared paste in a saucepan; add in the remaining ingredients and stir to combine well. Turn the heat to a simmer and let it cook, partially covered, for about 40 minutes or until the sauce has reduced to your desired consistency.
5. Bon appétit!

Sophisticated Cashew Mayonnaise

Servings: 12
Cooking Time: 10 Minutes
Ingredients:

- 3/4 cup raw cashews, soaked overnight and drained
- 2 tablespoons fresh lime juice
- 1/4 cup water
- 1/2 teaspoon deli mustard
- 1 teaspoon maple syrup
- 1/4 teaspoon garlic powder
- 1/4 teaspoon dried dill weed
- 1/2 teaspoon sea salt

Directions:

1. Blitz all the ingredients using a high-speed blender or food processor until smooth, creamy and uniform.
2. Add more spices, if needed.
3. Place in your refrigerator until ready to serve. Bon appétit!

Mediterranean Herb Ketchup

Servings: 8
Cooking Time: 30 Minutes
Ingredients:
- 1 tablespoon olive oil
- 16 ounces tomato paste
- 3 tablespoons brown sugar
- 1 teaspoon kosher salt
- 1/4 teaspoon ground cloves
- 1/4 teaspoon ground allspice
- 1 teaspoon dried basil
- 1 teaspoon dried oregano
- 1 teaspoon dried rosemary
- 1 teaspoon garlic powder
- 1 teaspoon onion powder
- 1 teaspoon porcini powder
- 3 tablespoons apple cider vinegar
- 1/4 cup water

Directions:
1. In a medium saucepan, heat the olive oil until sizzling.
2. Add in the remaining ingredients and bring to a simmer. Continue to simmer for about 25 minutes.
3. Process the mixture in your blender until smooth and uniform. Bon appétit!

Ligurian Walnut Sauce

Servings: 4
Cooking Time: 30 Minutes
Ingredients:
- 1/2 cup almond milk
- 1 slice white bread, crusts removed
- 1 cup raw walnuts
- 1/2 teaspoon garlic powder
- 1 teaspoon onion powder
- 1 teaspoon smoked paprika
- 2 tablespoons olive oil
- 1 tablespoon basil, chopped
- 3 curry leaves
- Sea salt and ground black pepper, to taste

Directions:
1. Put the almond milk and bread in a bowl and let it soak well.
2. Transfer the soaked bread to the bowl of your food processor or high-speed blender; add in the remaining ingredients.
3. Process until smooth, uniform and creamy.
4. Serve with pasta or zucchini noodles. Bon appétit!

Traditional Russian Chrain

Servings: 12
Cooking Time: 40 Minutes
Ingredients:

- 1 cup boiled water
- 6 ounces raw beets, peeled
- 1 tablespoon brown salt
- 9 ounces raw horseradish, peeled
- 1 tablespoon olive oil
- 1/2 cup apple cider vinegar

Directions:

1. In a heavy-bottomed saucepan, bring the water a boil. Then, cook the beets for about 35 minutes or until they have softened.
2. Remove the skins and transfer the beets to a food processor. Add in the remaining ingredients and blend until well combined.
3. Bon appétit!

Mexican-style Chili Sauce

Servings: 5
Cooking Time: 5 Minutes
Ingredients:

- 10 ounces canned tomato sauce
- 2 tablespoons apple cider vinegar
- 2 tablespoons brown sugar
- 1 Mexican chili pepper, minced
- 1/2 teaspoon dried Mexican oregano
- 1/4 teaspoon ground allspices
- Sea salt and ground black pepper, to taste

Directions:

1. In a mixing bowl, thoroughly combine all the ingredients.
2. Store in a glass jar in your refrigerator.
3. Bon appétit!

Traditional Balkan-style Ajvar

Servings: 6
Cooking Time: 30 Minutes
Ingredients:

- 4 red bell peppers
- 1 small eggplant
- 1 garlic clove, smashed
- 2 tablespoons olive oil
- 1 teaspoon white vinegar
- Kosher salt and ground black pepper, to taste

Directions:

1. Grill the peppers and eggplant until they are soft and charred.
2. Place the peppers in a plastic bag and let them steam for about 15 minutes. Remove the skin, seeds and core of the peppers and eggplant.
3. Then, transfer them to the bowl of your food processor. Add in the garlic, olive oil, vinegar, salt and black pepper and continue to blend until well combined.
4. Store in the refrigerator for up to 1 week. Bon appétit!

Dad's Homemade Ketchup

Servings: 12
Cooking Time: 30 Minutes
Ingredients:
- 2 tablespoons olive oil
- 1 onion, chopped
- 2 garlic cloves, chopped
- 1 teaspoon cayenne pepper
- 2 tablespoons tomato paste
- 30 ounces canned tomatoes, crushed
- 3 tablespoons brown sugar
- 1/4 cup apple cider vinegar
- Salt and fresh ground black pepper, to taste

Directions:
1. In a medium saucepan, heat the olive oil over a moderately high heat. Sauté the onions until tender and aromatic.
2. Add in the garlic and continue to sauté for 1 minute or until fragrant.
3. Add in the remaining ingredients and bring to a simmer. Continue to cook for about 25 minutes.
4. Process the mixture in your blender until smooth and uniform. Bon appétit!

Creamy Mustard Sauce

Servings: 4
Cooking Time: 35 Minutes
Ingredients:
- 1/2 plain hummus
- 1 teaspoon fresh garlic, minced
- 1 tablespoon deli mustard
- 1 tablespoon extra-virgin olive oil
- 1 tablespoon fresh lime juice
- 1 teaspoon red pepper flakes
- 1/2 teaspoon sea salt
- 1/4 teaspoon ground black pepper

Directions:
1. Thoroughly combine all ingredients in a mixing bowl.
2. Let it sit in your refrigerator for about 30 minutes before serving.
3. Bon appétit!

Classic Alfredo Sauce

Servings: 4
Cooking Time: 10 Minutes
Ingredients:
- 2 tablespoons olive oil
- 2 cloves garlic, minced
- 2 tablespoons rice flour
- 1 ½ cups rice milk, unsweetened
- Sea salt and ground black pepper, to taste
- 1/2 teaspoon red pepper flakes, crushed
- 4 tablespoons tahini
- 2 tablespoons nutritional yeast

Directions:
1. In a large saucepan, heat the olive oil over a moderate heat. Once hot, sauté the garlic for about 30 seconds or until fragrant.
2. Add in the rice flour and turn the heat to a simmer. Gradually add in the milk and continue to cook for a few minutes more, whisking constantly to avoid the lumps.
3. Add in the salt, black pepper, red pepper flakes, tahini and nutritional yeast.
4. Continue to cook on low until the sauce has thickened.
5. Store in an airtight container in your refrigerator for up to four days. Bon appétit!

Traditional French Sauce

Servings: 9
Cooking Time: 10 Minutes
Ingredients:

- 1 cup vegan mayonnaise
- 1 tablespoon fresh basil leaves, chopped
- 1 tablespoon fresh parsley leaves, chopped
- 1 tablespoon fresh scallions, chopped
- 3 small cornichon pickles, coarsely chopped
- 2 tablespoons capers, coarsely chopped
- 2 teaspoons fresh lemon juice
- 1 teaspoon Dijon mustard
- Sea salt and ground black pepper, to taste

Directions:

1. Thoroughly combine all ingredients in your food processor or blender.
2. Blend until uniform and creamy.
3. Bon appétit!

Vegan Barbecue Sauce

Servings: 10
Cooking Time: 25 Minutes
Ingredients:

- 1 cup tomato paste
- 2 tablespoons apple cider vinegar
- 2 tablespoons lime juice
- 1 tablespoon brown sugar
- 1 tablespoon mustard powder
- 1 teaspoon red pepper flakes, crushed
- 1 teaspoon onion powder
- 1 teaspoon garlic powder
- 1 teaspoon chili powder
- 2 tablespoons vegan Worcestershire
- 1/2 cup water

Directions:

1. Thoroughly combine all the ingredients in a saucepan over medium-high heat. Bring to a rolling boil.
2. Turn the heat to a bare simmer.
3. Let it simmer for about 20 minutes or until the sauce has reduced and thickened.
4. Place in your refrigerator for up to 3 weeks. Bon appétit!

Lime Coconut Sauce

Servings: 7
Cooking Time: 10 Minutes
Ingredients:

- 1 teaspoon coconut oil
- 1 large garlic clove, minced
- 1 teaspoon fresh ginger, minced
- 1 cup coconut milk
- 1 lime, freshly squeezed and zested
- A pinch of Himalayan rock salt

Directions:

1. In a small saucepan, melt the coconut oil over medium heat. Once hot, cook the garlic and ginger for about 1 minute or until aromatic.
2. Turn the heat to a simmer and add in the coconut milk, lime juice, lime zest and salt; continue to simmer for 1 minute or until heated through.
3. Bon appétit!

Spicy Cheese Sauce

Servings: 8
Cooking Time: 10 Minutes
Ingredients:
- 1/2 cup sunflower seeds, soaked overnight and drained
- 1/2 cup raw cashews, soaked overnight and drained
- 1 cup water
- 2 tablespoons lemon juice
- 1 tablespoon coconut oil
- 1/4 cup nutritional yeast
- 1 teaspoon hot sauce
- 1 teaspoon garlic powder
- 1/2 teaspoon curry powder
- Kosher salt and ground white pepper, to season

Directions:
1. Process the sunflower seeds, cashews and water in your blender until creamy and uniform.
2. Add in the remaining ingredients and continue to blend until everything is well incorporated.
3. Keep in your refrigerator for up to a week. Bon appétit!

Perfect Hollandaise Sauce

Servings: 6
Cooking Time: 15 Minutes
Ingredients:
- 1/2 cup cashews, soaked and drained
- 1 cup almond milk
- 2 tablespoons fresh lemon juice
- 3 tablespoons coconut oil
- 3 tablespoons nutritional yeast
- Sea salt and ground white pepper, to taste
- A pinch of grated nutmeg
- 1/2 teaspoon red pepper flakes, crushed

Directions:
1. Puree all the ingredients in a high-speed blender or food processor.
2. Then, heat the mixture in a small saucepan over low-medium heat; cook, stirring occasionally, until the sauce has reduced and thickened.
3. Bon appétit!

Easy Raw Pasta Sauce

Servings: 4
Cooking Time: 10 Minutes
Ingredients:
- 1 pound ripe tomatoes, cored
- 1 small onion, peeled
- 1 small garlic clove, minced
- 1 tablespoon fresh parsley leaves
- 1 tablespoon fresh basil leaves
- 1 tablespoon fresh rosemary leaves
- 4 tablespoons extra-virgin olive oil
- Sea salt and ground black pepper, to taste

Directions:
1. Blend all the ingredients in your food processor or blender until well combined.
2. Serve with warm pasta or zoodles (zucchini noodles).
3. Bon appétit!

Basic Tomato Sauce

Servings: 8
Cooking Time: 25 Minutes
Ingredients:

- 2 tablespoons olive oil
- 1 shallot, chopped
- 2 cloves garlic, minced
- 1 red chili pepper, seeded and minced
- 20 ounces canned tomatoes, puréed
- 2 tablespoons tomato paste
- 1 teaspoon cayenne pepper
- 1/2 teaspoon coarse sea salt

Directions:

1. In a medium saucepan, heat the olive oil over a moderately high heat. Sauté the shallot until tender and aromatic.
2. Add in the garlic and chili pepper; continue to sauté for 1 minute or until fragrant.
3. Add in the tomatoes, tomato paste, cayenne pepper and salt; turn the heat to a simmer. Continue to cook for about 22 minutes.
4. Bon appétit!

Authentic Béchamel Sauce

Servings: 5
Cooking Time: 10 Minutes
Ingredients:

- 2 tablespoons soy butter
- 2 tablespoons all-purpose flour
- 1 ½ cups oat milk
- Coarse sea salt, to taste
- 1/4 teaspoon turmeric powder
- 1/4 teaspoon ground black pepper, to taste
- A pinch of grated nutmeg

Directions:

1. Melt the soy butter in a sauté pan over a moderate flame. Add in the flour and continue to cook, whisking continuously to avoid lumps.
2. Pour the milk and continue whisking for about 4 minutes until the sauce has thickened.
3. Add in the spices and stir to combine well. Bon appétit!

Smoked Cheese Sauce

Servings: 6
Cooking Time: 10 Minutes
Ingredients:
- 1/2 cup raw cashews, soaked and drained
- 4 tablespoons water
- 2 tablespoons raw tahini
- Fresh juice of 1/2 lemon
- 1 tablespoon apple cider vinegar
- 2 carrots, cooked
- 1 teaspoon smoked paprika
- Sea salt, to taste
- 1 clove garlic
- 1 teaspoon fresh dill weed
- 1/2 cup frozen corn kernels, thawed and squeezed

Directions:
1. Process the cashews and water in your blender until creamy and uniform.
2. Add in the remaining ingredients and continue to blend until everything is well incorporated.
3. Keep in your refrigerator for up to a week. Bon appétit!

Almond And Sunflower Seed Mayo

Servings: 12
Cooking Time: 10 Minutes
Ingredients:
- 1/4 cup raw sunflower seeds, hulled
- 1/2 cup raw almonds
- 3/4 cup water
- 1/2 teaspoon onion powder
- 1/2 teaspoon garlic powder
- 1/4 teaspoon dried dill
- 1/2 teaspoon sea salt
- 1 cup sunflower seed oil
- 2 tablespoons fresh lime juice
- 1 tablespoon apple cider vinegar

Directions:
1. Process all the ingredients, except for the oil, in your blender or food processor until well combined.
2. Then, gradually add in the oil and continue to blend at low speed until smooth and creamy.
3. Add more spices, if needed.
4. Place in your refrigerator until ready to serve. Bon appétit!

Desserts & Sweet Treats

Raisin Oatmeal Biscuits

Servings:8
Cooking Time:20 Minutes
Ingredients:

- ½ cup plant butter
- 1 cup date sugar
- ¼ cup pineapple juice
- 1 cup whole-grain flour
- 1 tsp baking powder
- ½ tsp salt
- 1 tsp pure vanilla extract
- 1 cup old-fashioned oats
- ½ cup vegan chocolate chips
- ½ cup raisins

Directions:

1. Preheat oven to 370°F. Beat the butter and sugar in a bowl until creamy and fluffy. Pour in the juice and blend. Mix in flour, baking powder, salt, and vanilla. Stir in oats, chocolate chips, and raisins. Spread the dough on a baking sheet and bake for 15 minutes. Let completely cool on a rack.

Tangy Fruit Salad With Lemon Dressing

Servings: 4
Cooking Time: 15 Minutes
Ingredients:

- Salad:
- 1/2 pound mixed berries
- 1/2 pound apples, cored and diced
- 8 ounces red grapes
- 2 kiwis, peeled and diced
- 2 large oranges, peeled and sliced
- 2 bananas, sliced
- Lemon Dressing:
- 2 tablespoons fresh lemon juice
- 1 teaspoon fresh ginger, peeled and minced
- 4 tablespoons agave syrup

Directions:

1. Mix all the ingredients for the salad until well combined.
2. Then, in a small mixing bowl, whisk all the lemon dressing ingredients.
3. Dress your salad and serve well chilled. Bon appétit!

Tropical Bread Pudding

Servings: 5
Cooking Time: 2 Hours
Ingredients:
- 6 cups stale bread, cut into cubes
- 2 cups rice milk, sweetened
- 1/2 cup agave syrup
- 1 teaspoon vanilla extract
- 1/2 teaspoon ground cloves
- 1 teaspoon ground cinnamon
- 1/4 teaspoon coarse sea salt
- 5 tablespoons pineapple, crushed and drained
- 1 firm banana, sliced

Directions:
1. Place the bread cubes in a lightly oiled baking dish.
2. Now, blend the milk, agave syrup, vanilla, ground cloves, cinnamon and coarse sea salt until creamy and uniform.
3. Fold in the pineapple and banana and mix to combine well.
4. Spoon the mixture all over the bread cubes; press down slightly and set aside for about 1 hour.
5. Bake in the preheated oven at 350°F for about 1 hour or until the top of your pudding is golden brown.
6. Bon appétit!

Kiwi & Peanut Bars

Servings:9
Cooking Time:5 Minutes
Ingredients:
- 2 kiwis, mashed
- 1 tbsp maple syrup
- ½ tsp vanilla extract
- 2 cups old-fashioned rolled oats
- ½ tsp salt
- ¼ cup chopped peanuts

Directions:
1. Preheat oven to 360°F.
2. In a bowl, add kiwi, maple syrup, and vanilla and stir. Mix in oats, salt, and peanuts. Pour into a greased baking dish and bake for 25-30 minutes until crisp. Let completely cool and slice into bars to serve.

Easy Mocha Fudge

Servings: 20
Cooking Time: 1 Hour 10 Minutes
Ingredients:
- 1 cup cookies, crushed
- 1/2 cup almond butter
- 1/4 cup agave nectar
- 6 ounces dark chocolate, broken into chunks
- 1 teaspoon instant coffee
- A pinch of grated nutmeg
- A pinch of salt

Directions:
1. Line a large baking sheet with parchment paper.
2. Melt the chocolate in your microwave and add in the remaining ingredients; stir to combine well.
3. Scrape the batter into a parchment-lined baking sheet. Place it in your freezer for at least 1 hour to set.
4. Cut into squares and serve. Bon appétit!

Chocolate-glazed Cookies

Servings: 14
Cooking Time: 45 Minutes
Ingredients:

- 1/2 cup all-purpose flour
- 1/2 cup almond flour
- 1 teaspoon baking powder
- A pinch of sea salt
- A pinch of grated nutmeg
- 1/4 teaspoon ground cloves
- 1/2 cup cocoa powder
- 1/2 cup cashew butter
- 2 tablespoons almond milk
- 1 cup brown sugar
- 1 teaspoon vanilla paste
- 4 ounces vegan chocolate
- 1 ounce coconut oil

Directions:
1. In a mixing bowl, combine the flour, baking powder, salt, nutmeg, cloves and cocoa powder.
2. In another bowl, combine the cashew butter, almond milk, sugar and vanilla paste. Stir the wet mixture into the dry ingredients and stir until well combined.
3. Place the batter in your refrigerator for about 30 minutes. Shape the batter into small cookies and arrange them on a parchment-lined cookie pan.
4. Bake in the preheated oven at 330°F for approximately 10 minutes. Transfer the pan to a wire rack to cool slightly.
5. Microwave the chocolate until melted; mix the melted chocolate with the coconut oil. Spread the glaze over your cookies and let it cool completely. Bon appétit!

Raspberries Turmeric Panna Cotta

Servings:6
Cooking Time:10 Minutes + Chilling Time
Ingredients:

- ½ tbsp powdered vegetarian gelatin
- 2 cups coconut cream
- ¼ tsp vanilla extract
- 1 pinch turmeric powder
- 1 tbsp erythritol
- 1 tbsp chopped toasted pecans
- 12 fresh raspberries

Directions:
1. Mix gelatin and ½ tsp water and allow sitting to dissolve. Pour coconut cream, vanilla extract, turmeric, and erythritol into a saucepan and bring to a boil over medium heat, then simmer for 2 minutes. Turn the heat off. Stir in the gelatin until dissolved. Pour the mixture into 6 glasses, cover with plastic wrap, and refrigerate for 2 hours or more. Top with the pecans and raspberries and serve.

Sicilian Papaya Sorbet

Servings:4
Cooking Time:5 Minutes Freezing Time
Ingredients:

- 8 cups papaya chunks
- 2 limes, juiced and zested
- ½ cup pure date sugar

Directions:
1. Blend the papaya, lime juice, and sugar in a food processor until smooth. Transfer the mixture to a glass dish. Freeze for 2 hours. Take out from the freezer and scrape the top ice layer with a fork. Back to the freezer for 1 hour. Repeat the process a few more times until all the ice is scraped up. Serve frozen garnished with lime zest strips.

Berry Cupcakes With Cashew Cheese Icing

Servings:4
Cooking Time:35 Minutes + Cooling Time
Ingredients:

- 2 cups whole-wheat flour
- ¼ cup cornstarch
- 2 ½ tsp baking powder
- 1 ½ cups pure date sugar
- ½ tsp salt
- ¾ cup plant butter, softened
- 3 tsp vanilla extract
- 1 cup strawberries, pureed
- 1 cup oat milk, room temperature
- ¾ cup cashew cream
- 2 tbsp coconut oil, melted
- 3 tbsp pure maple syrup
- 1 tsp vanilla extract
- 1 tsp freshly squeezed lemon juice

Directions:

1. Preheat the oven to 350°F and line a 12-holed muffin tray with cupcake liners. Set aside.
2. In a bowl, mix flour, cornstarch, baking powder, date sugar, and salt. Whisk in plant butter, vanilla extract, strawberries, and oat milk until well combined. Divide the mixture into the muffin cups two-thirds way up and bake for 20-25 minutes. Allow cooling while you make the frosting.
3. In a blender, add cashew cream, coconut oil, maple syrup, vanilla, and lemon juice. Process until smooth. Pour the frosting into a medium bowl and chill for 30 minutes. Transfer the mixture into a piping bag and swirl mounds of the frosting onto the cupcakes. Serve immediately.

Vegan Cheesecake With Blueberries

Servings:6
Cooking Time:1 Hour 30 Minutes + Chilling Time
Ingredients:

- 2 oz plant butter
- 1 ¼ cups almond flour
- 3 tbsp Swerve sugar
- 1 tsp vanilla extract
- 3 tbsp flaxseed powder
- 2 cups cashew cream cheese
- ½ cup coconut cream
- 1 tsp lemon zest
- 2 oz fresh blueberries

Directions:

1. Preheat oven to 350°F and grease a springform pan with cooking spray. Line with parchment paper.
2. To make the crust, melt the plant butter in a skillet over low heat until nutty in flavor. Turn the heat off and stir in almond flour, 2 tbsp of Swerve sugar, and half of the vanilla until a dough forms. Press the mixture into the springform pan and bake for 8 minutes.
3. Mix flaxseed powder with 9 tbsp water and allow sitting for 5 minutes to thicken. In a bowl, combine cashew cream cheese, coconut cream, remaining Swerve sugar, lemon zest, remaining vanilla extract, and vegan "flax egg." Remove the crust from the oven and pour the mixture on top. Use a spatula to layer evenly. Bake the cake for 15 minutes at 400 °F. Then, reduce the heat to 230 °F and bake for 45-60 minutes. Remove to cool completely. Refrigerate overnight and scatter the blueberries on top. Serve.

Coconut & Chocolate Macaroons

Servings:4
Cooking Time:25 Minutes
Ingredients:
- 1 cup shredded coconut
- 2 tbsp cocoa powder
- 1 tbsp vanilla extract
- ⅔ cup coconut milk
- ¼ cup maple syrup
- A pinch of salt

Directions:
1. Preheat oven to 360°F.
2. Place the shredded coconut, cocoa powder, vanilla extract, coconut milk, maple syrup, and salt in a pot. Cook until a firm dough is formed. Shape balls out of the mixture. Arrange the balls on a lined with parchment paper baking sheet. Bake for 15 minutes. Allow cooling before serving.

Peanut Butter Oatmeal Bars

Servings: 20
Cooking Time: 25 Minutes
Ingredients:
- 1 cup vegan butter
- 3/4 cup coconut sugar
- 2 tablespoons applesauce
- 1 ¾ cups old-fashioned oats
- 1 teaspoon baking soda
- A pinch of sea salt
- A pinch of grated nutmeg
- 1 teaspoon pure vanilla extract
- 1 cup oat flour
- 1 cup all-purpose flour

Directions:
1. Begin by preheating your oven to 350°F.
2. In a mixing bowl, thoroughly combine the dry ingredients. In another bowl, combine the wet ingredients.
3. Then, stir the wet mixture into the dry ingredients; mix to combine well.
4. Spread the batter mixture in a parchment-lined square baking pan. Bake in the preheated oven for about 20 minutes. Enjoy!

Last-minute Macaroons

Servings: 10
Cooking Time: 15 Minutes
Ingredients:
- 3 cups coconut flakes, sweetened
- 9 ounces canned   coconut milk, sweetened
- 1 teaspoon ground anise
- 1 teaspoon vanilla extract

Directions:
1. Begin by preheating your oven to 325 °F. Line the cookie sheets with parchment paper.
2. Thoroughly combine all the ingredients until everything is well incorporated.
3. Use a cookie scoop to drop mounds of the batter onto the prepared cookie sheets.
4. Bake for about 11 minutes until they are lightly browned. Bon appétit!

Chocolate And Raisin Cookie Bars

Servings: 10
Cooking Time: 40 Minutes
Ingredients:

- 1/2 cup peanut butter, at room temperature
- 1 cup agave syrup
- 1 teaspoon pure vanilla extract
- 1/4 teaspoon kosher salt
- 2 cups almond flour
- 1 teaspoon baking soda
- 1 cup raisins
- 1 cup vegan chocolate, broken into chunks

Directions:

1. In a mixing bowl, thoroughly combine the peanut butter, agave syrup, vanilla and salt.
2. Gradually stir in the almond flour and baking soda and stir to combine. Add in the raisins and chocolate chunks and stir again.
3. Freeze for about 30 minutes and serve well chilled. Enjoy!

Chocolate Hazelnut Fudge

Servings: 20
Cooking Time: 1 Hour 10 Minutes
Ingredients:

- 1 cup cashew butter
- 1 cup fresh dates, pitted
- 1/4 cup cocoa powder
- 1/4 teaspoon ground cloves
- 1 teaspoon matcha powder
- 1 teaspoon vanilla extract
- 1/2 cup hazelnuts, coarsely chopped

Directions:

1. Process all ingredients in your blender until uniform and smooth.
2. Scrape the batter into a parchment-lined baking sheet. Place it in your freezer for at least 1 hour to set.
3. Cut into squares and serve. Bon appétit!

Pumpkin & Mango Lemon Cake

Servings:8
Cooking Time:60 Minutes
Ingredients:

- 1 ½ cups whole-grain flour
- ¾ cup pure date sugar
- ¼ cup yellow cornmeal
- 1 tsp baking soda
- ½ tsp salt
- ½ tsp baking powder
- ½ tsp ground cinnamon
- ½ tsp ground allspice
- ½ tsp ground ginger
- 1 cup pumpkin puree
- ⅓ cup canola oil
- 2 tsp grated lemon zest
- 2 tbsp water
- 1 mango, chopped

Directions:

1. Preheat oven to 360°F.
2. In a bowl, mix flour, sugar, cornmeal, baking soda, salt, baking powder, cinnamon, allspice, and ginger. In another bowl, whisk pumpkin puree, oil, lemon zest, and water until blend. Add in the mango. Pour the flour mixture into the pumpkin mixture and toss to coat. Pour the batter into a greased baking pan and bake for 45-50 minutes. Let cool before slicing.

Chocolate Peppermint Mousse

Servings:4
Cooking Time:10 Minutes + Chilling Time
Ingredients:
- ¼ cup Swerve sugar, divided
- 4 oz cashew cream cheese, softened
- 3 tbsp cocoa powder
- ¾ tsp peppermint extract
- ½ tsp vanilla extract
- 1/3 cup coconut cream

Directions:
1. Put 2 tablespoons of Swerve sugar, cashew cream cheese, and cocoa powder in a blender. Add the peppermint extract, ¼ cup warm water, and process until smooth. In a bowl, whip vanilla extract, coconut cream, and the remaining Swerve sugar using a whisk. Fetch out 5-6 tablespoons for garnishing. Fold in the cocoa mixture until thoroughly combined. Spoon the mousse into serving cups and chill in the fridge for 30 minutes. Garnish with the reserved whipped cream and serve.

Caribbean Pudding

Servings:4
Cooking Time:10 Minutes + Chilling Time
Ingredients:
- 3 kiwis, divided
- 1 can coconut milk
- ¼ cup organic cane sugar
- 1 tbsp cornstarch
- 1 tsp vanilla extract
- 2 pinches of salt
- 1 tbsp turmeric
- Ground cinnamon

Directions:
1. In a blender, place the 2 kiwis, coconut milk, sugar, cornstarch, vanilla, and salt. Blitz until smooth. Stir in turmeric. Pour into a pot. Bring to a boil, lower the heat and simmer for 3 minutes until pudding consistency is achieved. Remove to a bowl and let cool. Refrigerate covered overnight to set.
2. Before serving, cut the remaining kiwi into slices. In small glasses, put a layer of pudding, a layer of kiwi slices, a layer of pudding, and finish with kiwi slices. Serve sprinkled with cinnamon.

Poppy-granola Balls With Chocolate

Servings:8
Cooking Time:25 Minutes
Ingredients:
- ½ cup granola
- ¼ cup pure date sugar
- ½ cup golden raisins
- ½ cup shelled sunflower seeds
- ¼ cup poppy seeds
- 1 ½ cups creamy almond butter
- 2 cups vegan chocolate chips

Directions:
1. Blend the granola, sugar, raisins, sunflower seeds, and poppy seeds in a food processor. Stir in the almond butter and pulse until a smooth dough is formed. Leave in the fridge overnight. Shape small balls out of the mixture. Set aside.
2. Melt the chocolate in the microwave oven. Dip the balls into the melted chocolate and place on a baking sheet. Chill in the fridge for 30 minutes, until firm. Serve.

Baked Apples Filled With Nuts

Servings:4
Cooking Time:35 Minutes + Cooling Time
Ingredients:
- 4 gala apples
- 3 tbsp pure maple syrup
- 4 tbsp almond flour
- 6 tbsp pure date sugar
- 6 tbsp plant butter, cold and cubed
- 1 cup chopped mixed nuts

Directions:
1. Preheat the oven the 400 °F.
2. Slice off the top of the apples and use a melon baller or spoon to scoop out the cores of the apples. In a bowl, mix the maple syrup, almond flour, date sugar, butter, and nuts. Spoon the mixture into the apples and then bake in the oven for 25 minutes or until the nuts are golden brown on top and the apples soft. Remove the apples from the oven, allow cooling, and serve.

Avocado Truffles With Chocolate Coating

Servings:6
Cooking Time:5 Minutes
Ingredients:
- 1 ripe avocado, pitted
- ½ tsp vanilla extract
- ½ tsp lemon zest
- 5 oz dairy-free dark chocolate
- 1 tbsp coconut oil
- 1 tbsp unsweetened cocoa powder

Directions:
1. Scoop the pulp of the avocado into a bowl and mix with the vanilla using an immersion blender. Stir in the lemon zest and a pinch of salt. Pour the chocolate and coconut oil into a safe microwave bowl and melt in the microwave for 1 minute. Add to the avocado mixture and stir. Allow cooling to firm up a bit. Form balls out of the mix. Roll each ball in the cocoa powder and serve immediately.

Vanilla Cranberry & Almond Balls

Servings:12
Cooking Time:25 Minutes
Ingredients:
- 2 tbsp almond butter
- 2 tbsp maple syrup
- ¾ cup cooked millet
- ¼ cup sesame seeds, toasted
- 1 tbsp chia seeds
- ½ tsp almond extract
- Zest of 1 orange
- 1 tbsp dried cranberries
- ¼ cup ground almonds

Directions:
1. Whisk the almond butter and syrup in a bowl until creamy. Mix in millet, sesame seeds, chia seeds, almond extract, orange zest, cranberries, and almonds. Shape the mixture into balls and arrange on a parchment paper-lined baking sheet. Let chill in the fridge for 15 minutes.

Cardamom Coconut Fat Bombs

Servings:6
Cooking Time:10 Minutes
Ingredients:

- ½ cup grated coconut
- 3 oz plant butter, softened
- ¼ tsp green cardamom powder
- ½ tsp vanilla extract
- ¼ tsp cinnamon powder

Directions:

1. Pour the grated coconut into a skillet and roast until lightly brown. Set aside to cool. In a bowl, combine butter, half of the coconut, cardamom, vanilla, and cinnamon. Form balls from the mixture and roll each one in the remaining coconut. Refrigerate until ready to serve.

Easy Maple Rice Pudding

Servings:4
Cooking Time:30 Minutes
Ingredients:

- 1 cup short-grain brown rice
- 1 ¾ cups non-dairy milk
- 4 tbsp pure maple syrup
- 1 tsp vanilla extract
- A pinch of salt
- ¼ cup dates, pitted and chopped

Directions:

1. In a pot over medium heat, place the rice, milk, 1 ½ cups water, maple, vanilla, and salt. Bring to a boil, then reduce the heat. Cook for 20 minutes, stirring occasionally. Mix in dates and cook for another 5 minutes. Serve chilled in cups.

Layered Raspberry & Tofu Cups

Servings:4
Cooking Time:60 Minutes
Ingredients:

- ½ cup unsalted raw cashews
- 3 tbsp pure date sugar
- ½ cup soy milk
- ¾ cup firm silken tofu, drained
- 1 tsp vanilla extract
- 2 cups sliced raspberries
- 1 tsp fresh lemon juice
- Fresh mint leaves

Directions:

1. Grind the cashews and 3 tbsp of date sugar in a blender until a fine powder is obtained. Pour in soy milk and blitz until smooth. Add in tofu and vanilla and pulse until creamy. Remove to a bowl and refrigerate covered for 30 minutes.
2. In a bowl, mix the raspberries, lemon juice, and remaining date sugar. Let sit for 20 minutes. Assemble by alternating into small cups, one layer of raspberries, and one cashew cream layer, ending with the cashew cream. Serve garnished with mint leaves.

Raw Chocolate Mango Pie

Servings: 16
Cooking Time: 10 Minutes
Ingredients:

- Avocado layer:
- 3 ripe avocados, pitted and peeled
- A pinch of sea salt
- A pinch of ground anise
- 1/2 teaspoon vanilla paste
- 2 tablespoons coconut milk
- 5 tablespoons agave syrup
- 1/3 cup cocoa powder
- Crema layer:
- 1/3 cup almond butter
- 1/2 cup coconut cream
- 1 medium mango, peeled
- 1/2 coconut flakes
- 2 tablespoons agave syrup

Directions:
1. In your food processor, blend the avocado layer until smooth and uniform; reserve.
2. Then, blend the other layer in a separate bowl. Spoon the layers in a lightly oiled baking pan.
3. Transfer the cake to your freezer for about 3 hours. Store in your freezer. Bon appétit!

Chocolate Dream Balls

Servings: 8
Cooking Time: 10 Minutes
Ingredients:

- 3 tablespoons cocoa powder
- 8 fresh dates, pitted and soaked for 15 minutes
- 2 tablespoons tahini, at room temperature
- 1/2 teaspoon ground cinnamon
- 1/2 cup vegan chocolate, broken into chunks
- 1 tablespoon coconut oil, at room temperature

Directions:
1. Add the cocoa powder, dates, tahini and cinnamon to the bowl of your food processor. Process until the mixture forms a ball.
2. Use a cookie scoop to portion the mixture into 1-ounce portions. Roll the balls and refrigerate them for at least 30 minutes.
3. Meanwhile, microwave the chocolate until melted; add in the coconut oil and whisk to combine well.
4. Dip the chocolate balls in the coating and store them in your refrigerator until ready to serve. Bon appétit!

Vanilla Berry Tarts

Servings:4
Cooking Time:35 Minutes + Cooling Time
Ingredients:

- 4 tbsp flaxseed powder
- 1/3 cup whole-wheat flour
- ½ tsp salt
- ¼ cup plant butter, crumbled
- 3 tbsp pure malt syrup
- 6 oz cashew cream
- 6 tbsp pure date sugar
- ¾ tsp vanilla extract
- 1 cup mixed frozen berries

Directions:

1. Preheat oven to 350°F and grease mini pie pans with cooking spray. In a bowl, mix flaxseed powder with 12 tbsp water and allow soaking for 5 minutes. In a large bowl, combine flour and salt. Add in butter and whisk until crumbly. Pour in the vegan "flax egg" and malt syrup and mix until smooth dough forms. Flatten the dough on a flat surface, cover with plastic wrap, and refrigerate for 1 hour.

2. Dust a working surface with some flour, remove the dough onto the surface, and using a rolling pin, flatten the dough into a 1-inch diameter circle. Use a large cookie cutter, cut out rounds of the dough and fit into the pie pans. Use a knife to trim the edges of the pan. Lay a parchment paper on the dough cups, pour on some baking beans, and bake in the oven until golden brown, 15-20 minutes. Remove the pans from the oven, pour out the baking beans, and allow cooling. In a bowl, mix cashew cream, date sugar, and vanilla extract. Divide the mixture into the tart cups and top with berries. Serve.

Holiday Pecan Tart

Servings:4
Cooking Time:50 Minutes + Cooling Time
Ingredients:

- 4 tbsp flaxseed powder
- 1/3 cup whole-wheat flour
- ½ tsp salt
- ¼ cup cold plant butter, crumbled
- 3 tbsp pure malt syrup
- For the filling:
- 3 tbsp flaxseed powder + 9 tbsp water
- 2 cups toasted pecans, chopped
- 1 cup light corn syrup
- ½ cup pure date sugar
- 1 tbsp pure pomegranate molasses
- 4 tbsp plant butter, melted
- ½ tsp salt
- 2 tsp vanilla extract

Directions:

1. Preheat oven to 350°F. In a bowl, mix the flaxseed powder with 12 tbsp water and allow thickening for 5 minutes. Do this for the filling's vegan "flax egg" too in a separate bowl. In a bowl, combine flour and salt. Add in plant butter and whisk until crumbly. Pour in the crust's vegan "flax egg" and maple syrup and mix until smooth dough forms. Flatten the dough on a flat surface, cover with plastic wrap, and refrigerate for 1 hour. Dust a working surface with flour, remove the dough onto the surface, and using a rolling pin, flatten the dough into a 1-inch diameter circle. Lay the dough on a greased pie pan and press to fit the shape of the pan. Trim the edges of the pan. Lay a parchment paper on the dough, pour on some baking beans and bake for 20 minutes. Remove, pour out baking beans, and allow cooling.

2. In a bowl, mix the filling's vegan "flax egg," pecans, corn syrup, date sugar, pomegranate molasses, plant butter, salt, and vanilla. Pour and spread the mixture on the piecrust. Bake for 20 minutes or until the filling sets. Remove from the oven, decorate with more pecans, slice, and cool. Slice and serve.

Almond Granola Bars

Servings: 12
Cooking Time: 25 Minutes

Ingredients:

- 1/2 cup spelt flour
- 1/2 cup oat flour
- 1 cup rolled oats
- 1 teaspoon baking powder
- 1/2 teaspoon cinnamon
- 1/2 teaspoon ground cardamom
- 1/4 teaspoon freshly grated nutmeg
- 1/8 teaspoon kosher salt
- 1 cup almond milk
- 3 tablespoons agave syrup
- 1/2 cup peanut butter
- 1/2 cup applesauce
- 1/2 teaspoon pure almond extract
- 1/2 teaspoon pure vanilla extract
- 1/2 cup almonds, slivered

Directions:

1. Begin by preheating your oven to 350°F.
2. In a mixing bowl, thoroughly combine the flour, oats, baking powder and spices. In another bowl, combine the wet ingredients.
3. Then, stir the wet mixture into the dry ingredients; mix to combine well. Fold in the slivered almonds.
4. Scrape the batter mixture into a parchment-lined baking pan. Bake in the preheated oven for about 20 minutes. Let it cool on a wire rack. Cut into bars and enjoy!

30 day meal plan

Day 1
Breakfast: Spicy Vegetable And Chickpea Tofu Scramble
Lunch: Crispy Mushroom Wontons
Dinner: Rotini & Tomato Soup

Day 2
Breakfast: Pecan & Pumpkin Seed Oat Jars
Lunch: Hummus Avocado Boats
Dinner: Caribbean Lentil Stew

Day 3
Breakfast: Raspberry Almond Smoothie
Lunch: Rosemary And Garlic Roasted Carrots
Dinner: Vegetable & Black Bean Soup

Day 4
Breakfast: Banana-strawberry Smoothie
Lunch: Kale & Hummus Pinwheels
Dinner: Chicago-style Vegetable Stew

Day 5
Breakfast: Strawberry & Pecan Breakfast
Lunch: Silky Kohlrabi Puree
Dinner: Asian-style Bean Soup

Day 6
Breakfast: Broccoli Hash Browns
Lunch: Balkan-style Satarash
Dinner: Traditional Ukrainian Borscht

Day 7
Breakfast: Morning Oats With Walnuts And Currants
Lunch: Garlic And Herb Mushroom Skillet
Dinner: Cannellini Bean Soup With Kale

Day 8
Breakfast: Cinnamon Semolina Porridge
Lunch: Parmesan Baby Potatoes
Dinner:

Day 9
Breakfast: Classic Applesauce Pancakes With Coconut
Lunch: Tamari Lentil Dip
Dinner: Turmeric Bean Soup

Day 10
Breakfast: Traditional Spanish Tortilla
Lunch: Wine-braised Kale
Dinner: Quinoa And Black Bean Salad

Day 11
Breakfast: Almond Oatmeal Porridge
Lunch: Spinach, Chickpea And Garlic Crostini
Dinner: Daikon & Sweet Potato Soup

Day 12
Breakfast: Pumpkin Cake With Pistachios
Lunch: Four-seed Crackers
Dinner: Indian Chana Chaat Salad

Day 13
Breakfast: Buckwheat Porridge With Apples And Almonds
Lunch: Mexican-style Onion Rings
Dinner: Fennel & Corn Chowder

Day 14
Breakfast: Maple Banana Oats
Lunch: Greek-style Eggplant Skillet
Dinner: Greek-style Pinto Bean And Tomato Soup

Day 15

Breakfast: Morning Kasha With Mushrooms
Lunch: Spiced Roasted Cauliflower
Dinner: Lime Lentil Soup

Day 16

Breakfast: Thyme Pumpkin Stir-fry
Lunch: Za'atar Roasted Zucchini Sticks
Dinner: Spinach Soup With Gnocchi

Day 17

Breakfast: Berry Quinoa Bowl
Lunch: Chipotle Sweet Potato Fries
Dinner: Roasted Wild Mushroom Soup

Day 18

Breakfast: Chocolate-mango Quinoa Bowl
Lunch: Mustard Tofu-avocado Wraps
Dinner: Italian Nonna's Pizza Salad

Day 19

Breakfast: Creamy Sesame Bread
Lunch: Arugula & Hummus Pitas
Dinner: Vegetable Soup With Vermicelli

Day 20

Breakfast: Veggie Panini
Lunch: Thai Stir-fried Spinach
Dinner: Roasted Basil & Tomato Soup

Day 21

Breakfast: Vanilla Crepes With Berry Cream Compote Topping
Lunch: Bell Pepper & Seitan Balls
Dinner: Spicy Potato Soup

Day 22

Breakfast: Simple Apple Muffins
Lunch: Easy Zucchini Skillet
Dinner: Garlicky Broccoli Soup

Day 23

Breakfast: Amazing Yellow Smoothie
Lunch: Traditional Lebanese Mutabal
Dinner: Tofu Goulash Soup

Day 24

Breakfast: Coconut Fruit Smoothie
Lunch: Grilled Tofu Mayo Sandwiches
Dinner: Sudanese Veggie Stew

Day 25

Breakfast: Gingerbread Belgian Waffles
Lunch: Carrot Nori Rolls
Dinner: Rosemary Tomato Soup With Parmesan Croutons

Day 26

Breakfast: Tropical French Toasts
Lunch: Sweet Mashed Carrots
Dinner: Creamy Rutabaga Soup

Day 27

Breakfast: Classic French Toast
Lunch: Bell Pepper Boats With Mango Salsa
Dinner: Hearty Winter Quinoa Soup

Day 28

Breakfast: Fluffy Banana Pancakes
Lunch: Spicy Nut Burgers
Dinner: Italian Penne Pasta Salad

Day 29

Breakfast: Spicy Apple Pancakes
Lunch: Buttery Turnip Mash
Dinner: Green Bean & Rice Soup

Day 30

Breakfast: Vegan Banh Mi
Lunch: Spinach & Potato Soup
Dinner: Chickpea Garden Vegetable Medley

INDEX

Chipotle Sweet Potato Fries 29
Chocolate And Raisin Cookie Bars 83
Chocolate Dream Balls 87
Chocolate Hazelnut Fudge 83
Chocolate Peppermint Mousse 84
Chocolate Walnut Spread 63
Chocolate-glazed Cookies 80
Chocolate-mango Quinoa Bowl 17
Cinnamon Cashew Butter 66
Cinnamon Semolina Porridge 14
Classic Alfredo Sauce 73
Classic Applesauce Pancakes With Coconut 14
Classic French Toast 21
Coconut & Chocolate Macaroons 82
Coconut "feta" Cheese 69
Coconut Fruit Smoothie 20
Colorful Spelt Salad 54
Creamy Mustard Sauce 73
Creamy Rutabaga Soup 48
Creamy Sesame Bread 18
Crispy Mushroom Wontons 24
Crunchy Peanut Butter 64

D

Dad's Homemade Ketchup 73
Daikon & Sweet Potato Soup 40
Delicious Lemon Butter 69

E

Easy Maple Rice Pudding 86
Easy Mocha Fudge 79
Easy Raw Pasta Sauce 75
Easy Sweet Maize Meal Porridge 55
Easy Vegetable Pajeon 65
Easy Zucchini Skillet 32
Everyday Savory Grits 54

F

Fennel & Corn Chowder 40
Fluffy Banana Pancakes 22
Four-seed Crackers 28
Freekeh Salad With Za'atar 56

G

Garlic And Herb Mushroom Skillet 26
Garlicky Broccoli Soup 47
Gingerbread Belgian Waffles 20
Grandma's Pilau With Garden Vegetables 57
Greek-style Eggplant Skillet 28
Greek-style Pinto Bean And Tomato Soup 45
Green Bean & Rice Soup 44
Grilled Tofu Mayo Sandwiches 32

H

Hazelnut Snack 25
Healthy Chocolate Peanut Butter 66
Hearty Winter Quinoa Soup 43
Holiday Pecan Tart 88
Homemade Apple Butter 69
Hot Bean Dipping Sauce 53
Hummus Avocado Boats 24

I

Indian Chana Chaat Salad 44
Italian Bean Salad 62
Italian Nonna's Pizza Salad 46
Italian Penne Pasta Salad 49

K

Kale & Hummus Pinwheels 25
Kiwi & Peanut Bars 79

L

Last-minute Macaroons 82
Layered Raspberry & Tofu Cups 86
Ligurian Walnut Sauce 71
Lime Coconut Sauce 74
Lime Lentil Soup 41

M

Maple Banana Oats 16
Mediterranean Herb Ketchup 71
Mediterranean-style Rice 51
Mexican-style Chili Sauce 72
Mexican-style Onion Rings 28

Middle Eastern Za'atar Hummus 58
Millet Salad With Pine Nuts 54
Morning Kasha With Mushrooms 16
Morning Oats With Walnuts And Currants 14
Mustard Tofu-avocado Wraps 30

N

Nutty Chocolate Fudge Spread 68

O

Old-fashioned Chili 59
Old-fashioned Pecan Spread 67
Old-fashioned Sweet Potato Cakes 64
One-pot Italian Rice With Broccoli 53
Overnight Oatmeal With Prunes 60

P

Parmesan Baby Potatoes 26
Peanut Butter Oatmeal Bars 82
Pecan & Pumpkin Seed Oat Jars 12
Pecan And Apricot Butter 65
Perfect Hollandaise Sauce 75
Polenta With Mushrooms And Chickpeas 60
Poppy-granola Balls With Chocolate 84
Powerful Teff Bowl With Tahini Sauce 55
Pumpkin & Mango Lemon Cake 83
Pumpkin Cake With Pistachios 15

Q

Quick Everyday Chili 57
Quinoa And Black Bean Salad 39

R

Raisin Oatmeal Biscuits 78
Raspberries Turmeric Panna Cotta 80
Raspberry Almond Smoothie 12
Raspberry Star Anise Jelly 63
Raw Chocolate Mango Pie 87
Raw Mixed Berry Jam 65
Red Kidney Bean Patties 52
Red Pepper And Tomato Sauce 70
Roasted Basil & Tomato Soup 46

Roasted Pepper Spread 63
Roasted Wild Mushroom Soup 41
Rosemary And Garlic Roasted Carrots 24
Rosemary Tomato Soup With Parmesan Croutons 43
Rotini & Tomato Soup 35

S

Sicilian Papaya Sorbet 80
Silky Kohlrabi Puree 25
Simple Apple Muffins 19
Smoked Cheese Sauce 77
Sophisticated Cashew Mayonnaise 70
Spiced Cauliflower Bites 68
Spiced Roasted Cauliflower 29
Spiced Roasted Chickpeas 61
Spicy Apple Pancakes 22
Spicy Cheese Sauce 75
Spicy Nut Burgers 34
Spicy Potato Soup 42
Spicy Vegetable And Chickpea Tofu Scramble 12
Spinach & Potato Soup 35
Spinach Soup With Gnocchi 45
Spinach, Chickpea And Garlic Crostini 27
Split Pea And Potato Soup 55
Strawberry & Pecan Breakfast 13
Sudanese Veggie Stew 47
Sweet Cinnamon Walnut Spread 67
Sweet Cornbread Muffins 58
Sweet Mashed Carrots 33

T

Tamari Lentil Dip 27
Tangy Fruit Salad With Lemon Dressing 78
Teff Salad With Avocado And Beans 51
Thai Stir-fried Spinach 31
Thyme Pumpkin Stir-fry 17
Tofu Goulash Soup 42
Traditional Balkan-style Ajvar 72
Traditional French Sauce 74
Traditional Hanukkah Latkes 66
Traditional Lebanese Mutabal 32
Traditional Mnazaleh Stew 61
Traditional Russian Chrain 72
Traditional Spanish Tortilla 15
Traditional Tuscan Bean Stew (ribollita) 59

Traditional Ukrainian Borscht 39
Tropical Bread Pudding 79
Tropical French Toasts 21
Turmeric Bean Soup 38

V

Vanilla Berry Tarts 88
Vanilla Cranberry & Almond Balls 85
Vanilla Crepes With Berry Cream Compote Topping 19
Vegan Banh Mi 23
Vegan Barbecue Sauce 74
Vegan Cheesecake With Blueberries 81
Vegetable & Black Bean Soup 36
Vegetable Soup With Vermicelli 42
Veggie Panini 18

W

Wine-braised Kale 27

Z

Za'atar Roasted Zucchini Sticks 29

Printed in Great Britain
by Amazon

25040845R00057